WOMEN IN MINISTRY

WOMEN IN MINISTRY

Emerging Questions about the Diaconate

Phyllis Zagano

FOREWORD BY
William T. Ditewig

PAULIST PRESS
New York / Mahwah, NJ

Cover design by Sharyn Banks
Cover image of Phoebe © S. P. Wright. Used with permission.
Book design by Lynn Else

Library of Congress Cataloging-in-Publication Data

Zagano, Phyllis.
     Women in ministry : emerging questions about the diaconate / Phyllis Zagano ; foreword by William T. Ditewig.
         p. cm.
     Includes bibliographical references (p.   ).
     ISBN 978-0-8091-4756-4 (alk. paper) — ISBN 978-1-61643-132-7
1. Deaconesses—Catholic Church. 2. Ordination of women—Catholic Church. 3. Catholic Church—Clergy. 4. Women in the Catholic Church.
I. Title.
     BX1912.2.Z345 2012
     262`.142082—dc23

                                                                                          2011049044

Published by Paulist Press
997 Macarthur Boulevard
Mahwah, New Jersey 07430

www.paulistpress.com

Printed and bound in the
United States of America

CONTENTS

For Bill Ditewig

FOREWORD

Long before the dramatic ecclesial event known as the Second Vatican Council, the landscape of ministry within the Catholic Church, including ordained and official ministries, was in a state of considerable tension, challenge, and opportunity. The emergence of new nation-states—along with the concomitant restructuring of the political and social orders resulting from the Enlightenment, political and economic revolutions, and massive demographic shifts due to tidal waves of emigration and immigration—followed by fifty years of world wars, worldwide economic collapse, the rise of totalitarian regimes, the Shoah, and the beginning of the nuclear age and cold war: all of these things and more demanded that all Christians, and Catholics in particular, examine who we are and how we relate to the explosively complex world in which we live. In short, how do we continue to serve and preach the Good News of Jesus the Christ effectively in a world more in need of it than ever?

This was the central question facing the 2,640 bishops who assembled under the leadership of Pope John XXIII on October 11, 1962, to begin the Second Vatican Council. The bishops carried with them their own insights, experiences, cultures, and battle scars into the Council aula, and although it took them some time to mature in their own understanding of the task at hand, they realized that what they were doing was trying to build on the solid foundation of Tradition a new ecclesial reality, one that would work to transform the world into a place in which such tragedies and cruelty could no longer take place, a world truly transformed in the light of Christ through the presence and action of the Spirit.

The bishops began to speak of a "new way of thinking" (*novus mentis habitus*), and this expression was repeated several times by popes Paul VI and John Paul II. This new way of thinking was to inform the Church's self-vision and her mission. This new way of thinking was to focus on service, not power. Furthermore, Paul VI, in his closing address to the Council on December 7, 1965, reminded the Fathers: "We stress that the teaching of the Council is channeled in one direction, the service of humankind, of every condition, in every weakness and need. The Church has declared herself a servant of humanity...[and] the idea of service has been central."[1] And it was this same pope who connected the dots about this ecclesial service when he enacted the Council's decision to renew a permanent diaconate in the Latin Church, and wrote that this renewed diaconate is a "driving force for the Church's *diakonia* and a sacrament of the Lord Christ himself, who 'came not to be served but to serve.'"[2] John Paul II would echo this insight when he observed that "the service of the deacon is the Church's service sacramentalized."[3]

The nature and role of the renewed diaconate had been in a state of constant examination before the Council began, but it took on particular focus after the Council and Pope Paul VI's decisions on the matter. Suddenly there was again a major order of ordained ministry that did not find its sacramental end in eventual ordination to the presbyterate, an almost explosive shift of ministerial paradigm, in which for more than a millennium all ordinations to minor and major orders pointed inexorably to the presbyterate. Now, not only could a candidate (male) be ordained to the diaconate without proceeding to the presybterate, but that candidate could also be either celibate or married.

The question of ordaining women was raised by a number of bishops prior to the Council, and in the research done on the diaconate prior to the Council, considerable attention had been given to the question of the possibility and desirability of doing so. Although ultimately this question was not addressed during the Council, the theology of the diaconate itself was addressed, with Cardinal Suenens of Belgium making a number of important points. First, he pointed to history, citing the authority of Scripture, the apostolic Fathers, constant tradition, and the liturgical books of East and West, all of which testify to the diaconate. Second, he spoke of the many charisms given to the Church in addition to the priesthood, charisms that were used to provide direct service to the bishop, especially in the care of the poor and the nurturing of the community. He remarked that even though many of these tasks could be given to laypersons, this did not mean that the diaconate was not needed. According to Suenens, these tasks should be given only to persons (ordained or not) who have the necessary charisms, and the Church herself has a right to the benefit of all the graces given to her by God, and one of those graces is the diaconate. In other words, ordination as a deacon is about the giftedness of the Church, not merely a "transfer of power" to a particular individual.[4]

I have offered this background as a bridge to the invaluable work of Phyllis Zagano. As the Church continues to examine the nature and role of the diaconate, we realize very clearly that the diaconate—as an order—is the most malleable and adaptable to the needs of the Church and the world. The diaconate is related to, but distinct from, the presbyterate, and this fact needs to be explored more systematically. For more than a millennium, the diaconate was viewed as a partial and transitory participation in the priesthood; now we realize that the diaconate stands on its own and does not identify itself only in reference to the priesthood. This frees our reflection from the priesthood itself and opens up additional channels of dialogue and research. Challenged by the Council to a "new way of thinking" and constantly, as *Gaudium et Specs* says, to "read the signs of the times in light of the Gospel," the Church must reflect critically on her own giftedness in addressing these signs of the times in new and creative ways. The gifts of women as full partners in the life of the Church need to be nurtured and appreciated. Dr. Zagano's work documents, inspires, and challenges our understanding of ministry itself. If we are called to be a Servant Church (as proclaimed by Paul VI), then we must follow Cardinal Suenens' example and ask ourselves, Who is already ministering in a diaconal way in the Church? Suenens would say that we should ordain those people who are already performing diaconal service in the Church, and no one could deny that women throughout our history have been the servant-leaders of the Church. Dr. Zagano picks up on these themes and offers us a framework from which to re-vision the ecclesial role of women.

In these seminal articles assembled together for the first time, Dr. Zagano reviews the parameters of this new vision: What are the lessons we can draw from history, from ecumenical dialogues, from theology and the liturgy? Anyone interested in the future of ministry in the Church emerging in the twenty-first century needs to wrestle with these issues. Just as the bishops of the Second Vatican

Council brought their own experiences of tragedy, war, and devastation into the aula for debate and discussion to craft a new way of responding to the world, so too must we now bring to the table our own challenges, including, for example, ethnic cleansing, the reality of clerical abuse, the loss of credibility in ecclesial leadership, the opportunities of technology and globalization, and so many more. Through the landmark work of scholars such as Phyllis Zagano, we can perhaps craft new wineskins to carry the new wine of salvation to future generations. The question before us is the same as that which faced the bishops at Vatican II: How do we continue to serve and preach the Good News of Jesus the Christ effectively in a world more in need of it than ever?

William T. Ditewig
Diocese of Monterey, California

ACKNOWLEDGMENTS

To whom am I indebted? As I turn this question over and over, a parade of friends, acquaintances, relatives, and librarians (always, the librarians) crosses before me in my mind. To thank them all is not possible, but in justice I can attempt to name most of those who helped with the creation of this book as it moved from invited lectures and talks, to refereed academic articles, to the present manuscript prepared during my term as visiting professor of theology and religion at Saint Leo University, Florida.

Chapter 1, "Women and the Church: Unfinished Business of Vatican II," began as a combination of lectures presented at the 2005 annual meeting of the Catholic Theological Society of America in Saint Louis, to which I was invited by William Clark, SJ, and at Saint Mary's College, South Bend, Indiana, at the invitation of Kathleen Dolphin, PBVM. It was later published by *Horizons* (Villanova University), the Journal of the College Theology Society, through the good offices of its editor, Anthony J. Godzeiba, and of Irene C. Noble, the editorial assistant of the journal.

Chapter 2, "Catholic Women's Ordination: The Ecumenical Implications of Women Deacons in the Armenian Apostolic Church, the Orthodox Church of Greece, and Union of Utrecht Old Catholic Churches," originally appeared in the *Journal of Ecumenical Studies* (Temple University), through the offices of Nancy E. Krody, managing editor, and was later presented as corrected at the National Workshop on Christian Unity/Catholic Association of Diocesan Ecumenical and Interreligious Officers meeting, in Tampa, Florida.

Chapter 3, "The Question of Governance and Ministry for Women," grew from talks given at Regis University, Denver, Colorado, at the invitation of Thomas Leininger, and at the annual meeting of Voice of the Faithful of Long Island in 2006, before it appeared in *Theological Studies* (Marquette University), with the careful editing of David G. Schultenover, SJ.

The papers as originally published have been edited and modified to conform with Paulist Press's house style.

Throughout the years of research and preparation of these papers and, now, book, I have depended upon the generosity of many colleagues across the nation, whose enthusiastic response to my ideas about the restoration of the female diaconate in the Catholic Church has both cheered me and helped light my path. To each and every person who assisted me as I checked and rechecked footnotes and facts, I send notice of my large debt of gratitude. As the circle of colleagues spreads farther from Hofstra University and my home Diocese of Rockville Centre, I fear I risk forgetting or omitting one or another. But, to the librarians and library staff of Hofstra University; to Sheila Browne, RSM, director, Office of Worship, and Msgr. Donald Beckmann, director, Office of Ecumenical and Interreligious Affairs of the Diocese of Rockville Centre; to Fr. Krikor Maksoudian, the Armenian Church, Diocese of America; to Rev. John E. Fanning, JCD; to Terrence W. Tilley, Fordham University; to Maureen Tilley, Fordham University; to Miriam Therese Winter, MMS, Hartford Seminary; to Ron Roberson, CSP, assistant director of the U.S. Conference of Catholic Bishops

Acknowledgments

Secretariat for Ecumenical and Interreligious Affairs; to Mary Gautier, Center for Applied Research in the Apostolate, Georgetown University; to C. Kevin Gillespie, SJ, now at Loyola University, Chicago; to David DeLambo, Office of Planning, Diocese of Cleveland; to John F. Kane, Regis University, Denver; to Gary Macy, Santa Clara University; and to Robert F. Taft, SJ, Emeritus Professor of Eastern Liturgy at the Pontifical Oriental Institute, Rome— I send forth thanks for your encouragement and assistance. My apologies if I have forgotten anyone.

I had the space and time to edit and recheck this manuscript during my time as a visiting professor at Saint Leo University, Florida, where I enjoyed the cheerful collegiality of many colleagues, especially Michael W. Cooper, SJ; W. Thomas Poynor; Michael J. Tkacik; and Randall J. Woodard; the help of fine librarians, especially Carol Ann Moon and Deidre Selwyn; the technical assistance of computing specialists, especially Eric Maule; and the generosity and good cheer of the Benedictine Sisters of Florida, at whose Holy Name Priory I lived during this visiting semester.

I depended all along on the personal support of my family and many other colleagues and friends who have also lent an eye to my manuscripts, especially Peter J. Houle and Irene Kelly, RSHM.

Finally, with heartfelt thanks, both for his invitation to come to Saint Leo for a semester, and for his encouragement and assistance in my work on the diaconate, I am delighted to have the opportunity to dedicate a book—this book—to Deacon William T. Ditewig, and to wish him fair winds and following seas in all his endeavors.

April 29, 2010
Saint Leo University, Florida

CHAPTER ONE

WOMEN AND THE CHURCH

Unfinished Business of Vatican II

The bright hope that shone in the Catholic Church as the Second Vatican Council came to a close now wears almost a fifty-year tarnish, as the facts of the unfinished business relating to women are increasingly recognized. There was hope, genuine hope, that women would become equal partners in the lives and ministries of the ordained, even that they would be restored to the dignity of office and order, as the ebullience of the late 1960s spilled into Saint Peter's Square. The closing words of Vatican II regarding women seemed promising:

> The hour is coming, in fact has come, when the vocation of women is being acknowledged in its fullness, the hour in which women acquire in the world an influence, an effect and a power never hitherto achieved. That is why, at this moment when the human race is undergoing so deep a transformation, women imbued with a spirit of the Gospel can do so much to aid humanity in not falling.[1]

In those waning days of 1965, hope lit the future. What would it bring? Would women become the legitimate wives of priests in the Latin Church? Would women be ordained to the diaconate, and to the priesthood? Would women have real input in the formation of doctrine?

The excitement has faded, and women are still on the outside looking in wherever the power and authority of governance and jurisdiction are involved. The neuralgic issues of sex and gender as they have been considered by the Catholic Church over the past fifty years seem no closer to any hierarchically approved solution, but Catholic women have made their own determinations about each. Women's voices continue to be raised, both organizationally and individually. Catholic organizations as diverse as Voice of the Faithful (VOTF), the Leadership Conference of Women Religious (LCWR), and Call to Action (CTA) press women-related questions to the fore.[2] Individually, women belong to the growing cadre of Catholic lay ministers and theologians, and by some estimates there are over 24,000 women lay ministers in the United States alone.[3]

The presence and force of women in theology and ministry press forward three interrelated questions about women and the Church: (1) married clergy, especially a married presbyterate; (2) women's ordination, especially women deacons; and (3) lay participation in the power and authority of governance and jurisdiction. Each flows from the unfulfilled hopes of Vatican II, staunched as they are by the determined resistance of Catholic hierarchy to either share power or to enlarge the classes of persons who hold the power and authority of governance and jurisdiction.

Two of these questions—married clergy (priests and deacons) and lay involvement in governance and jurisdiction—reflect upon each other. Both married clergy and a greater role for the laity—that is, a sharing in power and authority—might provide the leaven for the Catholic hierarchy to better understand the ways in which women's responses to the needs and desires of the whole Church could be expanded within the current structures.

MARRIED CLERGY

The largest cadre of married clergy in the Church comprises the married men among the more than 30,000 deacons worldwide.[4] The next largest cadre comprises married Eastern Catholic priests.[5] The smallest cadre by far comprises married Roman Catholic priests in union with Rome, nearly all converts from other Christian denominations or churches.

While the Second Vatican Council did not directly discuss the restoration of the tradition of ordaining married men to priesthood in the West, a married priesthood was a topic of several interventions during the Twenty-first Synod of Catholic Bishops on the Eucharist in 2005.[6] Today, hundreds of resigned priests remain out of official ministry, while hundreds of other qualified men do not choose presbyteral life in the Latin Church, specifically because of the legal requirement of celibacy. Many organizations, including the Corps of Reserved Priests United for Service (CORPUS), Celibacy is the Issue Ministries (CITI), and Rent-a-Priest,[7] form loci for discussion and extra-ecclesial ministry by the approximately 25,000 resigned priests in the United States. The International Federation of Married Catholic Priests does much the same for the approximately 120,000 resigned priests worldwide. Married Priests Now! is headed by former Zambian Archbishop Emmanuel Milingo (b. 1930), who married a Korean acupuncturist in a Unification Church ceremony led by Sun Myung Moon in 2001. Milingo briefly reconciled with the Vatican, but then slipped out of Rome in

June 2006 with former Washington, DC, priest George Augustus Stallings, Jr., patriarch and founder of the African American Catholic Congregation. Milingo has ordained several married men as priests, and ordained four men as bishops in the United States in September 2006.

Other organizations, such as FutureChurch[8] in the United States and Catholic Women's Ordination in the United Kingdom, mount campaigns and provide information in support of a married priesthood, women deacons, and women priests, much as www.womenpriests.org does on an international level.

Despite Rome's acceptance of convert married clergy (mostly former Episcopalians in the United States), an increasing restiveness among Eastern Catholics (whose bishops in North America had Western custom imposed upon them in 1929, but who are quietly ignoring that agreement),[9] and wider calls from Roman Catholic presbyterates (and some bishops) to allow a married priesthood, there is little official response or movement to meet their requests. The 2005 Synod on the Eucharist deflected and countered multiple calls both inside and outside the Synod for genuine discussion on the matter, although some pointed statements argued on behalf of the ordination of married men as priests.

In addition to the approximately three hundred resigned married priests listed with CITI Ministries who perform marriage ceremonies under civil authority, there are multiple "Catholic" communions in the United States whose ministers also baptize, celebrate Eucharist, and make themselves known in more or less public ways as Catholic priests.[10] The fact that these bodies claim increasing validity through a number of ways, not the least of which is public acceptance of their various ministries and ministerial actions, presents a problem of authority for Catholic hierarchs, who have depended on the implicit obedience of even laicized priests, whose rescripts of laicization include their exclusion from any public ministry in the Church.

Some rescripts granting "reduction to the lay state" retain the requirement of celibacy. Laicized bishops in particular are not permitted to marry. (Former priests are permitted, even required, to provide absolution in emergency situations.) A number of functioning former Catholic priests are in a canonical quagmire. Without explicit permission to marry they cannot validly contract a Catholic marriage. Yet they are married. They do not have faculties from a Catholic bishop, but the sacraments they perform are valid. As with CITI Ministries, some meet civil state and local requirements as marriage ministers, and/or gain legitimacy by affiliation with one of the many Catholic communions that trace their apostolic lineage through Union of Utrecht Catholic bishops.

The details of what Rome considers necessary for a Church to be in communion with the Catholic Church (essentially, acceptance of papal authority and a valid provenance of orders) escape many people. From these requirements flow the restrictions on alternative clergy. Increasingly, however, ordinary Catholics do not accept the multiple restrictions on priesthood, and this is reflected in their willingness to ignore canon law in the name of ministry.[11] Catholics are willing to accept married priests, even if the provenance of their orders or the legitimacy of their status can be challenged by the diocesan bishop, and many actually do not care whether or not the traditional restrictions apply. So the impetus toward a wider married priesthood, begun with the conversion of married ministers from other traditions and enhanced by the restoration of Eastern Catholic traditions in the United States, melds into a situation whereby it appears that individual Catholics are unconcerned whether Church authority—in the person of the diocesan bishop—has anything to do or say about the ministry at hand. This is not in the least a leap of logic. It reflects both a growing ignorance of Catholics for whom Catholicism is a cultural base, but not an organized system of belief, and a disregard for the authority of an often-discredited and disrespected episcopacy.[12]

LAY INVOLVEMENT

The official resistance to a wider married priesthood in the Catholic Church underscores the Church's official stance relative to the status of women, all of whom are lay members of the Church. Women's input to doctrine and policy is severely limited by several factors, not the least of which is refusal to allow them into the clerical state. The more serious problem, however, remains to be an apparent psychosexual dysfunction on the part of too many Catholic clergy (especially those in positions of authority) on the matter of women. The automatic negative response to the writings of some women theologians, even and especially those whose writings are clearly within dogmatic and doctrinal limits, bespeaks a serious—and contagious—condition in the Church, which might or might not begin to be cured by more numerous and more visible married priests.[13]

But clericalism extends to and is extended by all laymen and laywomen who have allowed it to co-opt them and their thought. There are laypersons serving in advisory capacities at every level of Church governance, and there are even laypersons who hold office (albeit with limited powers) in diocesan structures. Whether as volunteers or as lay employees, insofar as laymen and laywomen "know their places," they are permitted to contribute at various levels of Vatican, diocesan, and even parish bureaucracy. The governance and responsibility over Church finances provides one example. While canon law requires every diocese and parish to have a finance council, the council is chosen by the diocesan bishop or the pastor and is wholly advisory.[14]

Precisely because they are not clerics, neither laymen nor laywomen can canonically "share" the power of governance; they may only "cooperate" in its exercise. It is telling that the word *share* was replaced by *cooperate* in the drafting of the 1983 Code of Canon Law, resulting in the power of governance being restricted to clerics. This is key to understanding canon 129, which presents the distinction between those in "sacred orders" and "lay members of the Christian faithful":

1. Those who have received sacred orders are qualified, according to the norm of the prescripts of the law, for the power of governance, which exists in the Church by divine institution and is also called the power of jurisdiction.
2. Lay members of the Christian faithful can cooperate in the exercise of this same power according to the norm of law.[15]

Canon 129 clearly indicates that the ordained, by virtue of their ordination, are qualified for authority and governance; by implication, the nonordained are not. Recall, presently there are no women ordained in the Catholic Church.

On one level, the restriction of juridical power to the ordained may be a problem both of sex and of gender. Married men, including and especially married men who are legitimate priests in the Latin Church (typically former Episcopal priests), find themselves officially and unofficially marginalized. Married Latin priests typically may not exercise the "care of souls," that is, cannot become pastors, and so cannot have the jurisdiction that comes with the pastorate, although some carry the title "priest in charge" of a parish, which must canonically have a celibate priest pastor.[16] Similarly, women, laymen, and deacons cannot be pastors, but rather can serve as administrators of parishes through the provisions of canon 517, which provides there must be a canonical (priest) pastor.

Because of such marginalization, laymen and laywomen can say and do little to change the Church from within, even though they are in the majority of the Christian faithful. There are 69 million Catholics in the United States and over a billion worldwide. In the United States, there are 42,000 priests, over 15,000 deacons, and approximately 72,000 men and women religious.[17] Yet large numbers of laymen and laywomen (including religious sisters) are publicly exasperated by the various scandals involving sexual and financial malfeasance on the part of clergy at every level, and their distress and dismay are taking their toll on the bottom lines of parish and diocesan financial statements. Unfortunately, the removal of funds from the systems with which they disagree will not change the systems. The removal of funds from the systems will only cut down on the charitable works of the diocese or parish involved and could cause other laymen and laywomen, including women religious, to lose their paid positions.

WOMEN'S ORDINATION TO THE DIACONATE

Recent confluences of scholarship and activism have split the issues of women priests and women deacons, establishing both a new scholarly and a new public argument for each.[18] After Vatican II, Pope Paul VI issued his *motu proprio Sacrum Diaconatus Ordinem* (June 18, 1967), restoring the permanent diaconate. He later asked the obvious question following the publication of his *motu proprio Ad Pascendum* (August 15, 1972), which further restored the permanent diaconate in the Latin Church: Could women be ordained to the diaconate? That question was soon overshadowed by its companion question: Could women be ordained to the priesthood? Despite two Vatican documents on priesthood (the Declaration by the Congregation for the Doctrine of the Faith, *Inter Insigniores* [October 15, 1976] and Pope John Paul's apostolic letter *Ordinatio Sacerdotalis* [May 22, 1994]), no definitive statement has been rendered on the question of the ordination of women.[19] The Congregation for the Doctrine of the Faith did issue an opinion that the teaching on women priests was part of the magisterium, but that was the opinion of a curial office, not a formal papal declaration of infallibility. Nothing is infallibly stated unless it is clearly defined as such.[20]

The objection of the curial opinion of 1976, that a woman cannot represent Christ (an objection understood by most scholars as a naive physicalism), was dropped from the 1994 papal document, which retained the objection from authority (Jesus chose men). This objection does not apply to the diaconate.

It is not useful to conflate the questions of priesthood and diaconate for many reasons, not the least of which is the fact that the remaining objection in *Ordinatio Sacerdotalis*, even if true, does not apply to the diaconate, since the apostles—not Jesus—chose the first deacons.[21] Both statements leave the matter of the ordination of women deacons aside.

The most recent Vatican statement on women deacons is a 2002 document of the International Theological Commission (ITC), published in English as *From Diakonia of Christ to the Diakonia of the Apostles*.[22] This document stops short of denying Catholic women in the West reentry to the ordained diaconate, and makes no real argument against the return to tradition. Neither does this document effectively counter the historical status of the many women to whom Pope John Paul II pointed in *Mulieris Dignitatem* as cooperators and helpers in the ministry of Jesus and the apostles— Phoebe, Prisca, Euodia, Mary, and others who "played an active and important role in the life of the early Church."[23] Many of these women effectively had pastoral care of local ecclesial communities. Whether they are retroactively considered "lay" or "clergy," revisionist history presented at any level of the Church cannot rewrite the present belief and understanding that women can (and do) so minister again.

Scripture alone will not convince Catholic hierarchy that women can be ordained as priests, especially not in the pontificate of Benedict XVI. Writing in the *Harvard Divinity Bulletin*, Francis Fiorenza recalled the beliefs of Joseph Ratzinger as a professor on the faculty at Munich while Fiorenza was a student:

> Elisabeth [Schüssler] was completing a dissertation on those passages of the New Testament texts that are the classical sources for the "priesthood of the faithful." Arguing from New Testament affirmations that all believers are priests, she pointed to the possibility of the full ministry of women in the church. She and Ratzinger argued rather vigorously and at length. Whenever Elisabeth made a point, Ratzinger graciously smiled, as he often did and does, and conceded that her exegesis of the biblical texts was correct, but

he maintained that the Roman Catholic position could not orient itself so primarily on scripture without taking account of the teaching authority of the church. In distinction to other faculty members, Ratzinger was adamant against the ordination of women—a position that he maintains today.[24]

That Benedict XVI maintains this position is clear. But since the magisterial teaching of the Church is defined as the definitive exegesis of both Scripture and Tradition, it would seem impossible for the one to come in collision with the other. The intransigence of Benedict XVI on the point of women as priests is well known. But as a historian, Benedict cannot deny the history of the ordination of women as deacons.

Part of the difficulty in the historical analysis of women ministers, of course, is that some of these women ministered alongside their husbands.[25] In fact, as the present issues of women priests and women deacons continue to separate, the question of the current status of deacons' wives comes to the fore. In current practice in the United States and elsewhere, deacons' wives are often required to train and sometimes co-minister with their husbands, even thought they are not permitted to be ordained.

Hence, aside from scholars and others who propose the ordination of women, the largest single cadre of supporters of the concept of ordaining women deacons might be comprised of married men, including married Catholic clergy, who might well lead the way for the restoration of the female diaconate in the Church (East and West), and specifically for the restoration of a ministerial—as opposed to a monastic—female diaconate.[26]

The implications of the restoration of the female diaconate are multifold. The usual argument is that women deacons henceforth could become priests. Continued scholarship supports the historical facts of the ordination of women deacons and contemporary churches in "imperfect communion" with the Catholic Church—including those whose sacraments and orders are recognized as valid by Rome—have restored the female diaconate. So, with mounting pressure to recognize the "ordainability" of women, contrary arguments mount as well.

But the argument that women cannot be ordained deacons because such implies women priests becomes an argument *for* the ordination of women as priests. That is, if women were already ordained deacons, and are being ordained deacons, then women may also have been ordained priests and can be so ordained again.[27] However, there is no direct link between ordaining a woman as deacon and ordaining a woman as priest, except for the conflation of the diaconate into the priesthood in the West, and the concurrent reduction of the diaconate to a step on the way to priesthood. In other words, the permanent diaconate—of men or of women—is just that. Diaconal ordination does not imply priestly ordination.

The need for women deacons is critical in the debate over women's ordination. In 1980, the discussion of what came to be canon 517.2 of the new (1983) Code of Canon Law[28]—the provision allowing deacons or groups of religious effectively to have pastoral care of parishes—enjoyed the intervention of Cardinal Rosalio José Castillo Lara, SDB, then secretary of the Roman Curia, who described his positive experience of the pastoral ministry by women religious in his vicariate in Venezuela. In effect, he was using women religious as deacons. His intervention led directly to the inclusion of this new canon in the 1983 Code. Other bishops of Latin America and South America have since enjoyed the same ministerial assistance of communities of women religious in response to their priest shortages.[29]

Fired by the Second Vatican Council even twenty years after it closed, simultaneous discussion of ministry by women took place around the world. In the United States, from 1983 to 1992, an ad hoc committee of the U.S. Conference of Catholic Bishops led by Bishop Joseph Imesh prepared four drafts of a letter on women in the Church entitled "One in Christ Jesus," which included in its first two drafts the suggestion that women could be "installed" to the diaconate. The clear implication was that women would be able to become—somehow—deacons.[30] But women "installed" as deacons would not be clerics. They would still be laypersons.

Even the notion of women "installed" to the diaconate evaporated as the U.S. bishops' letter turned into a statement of response to and affirmation of the 1994 apostolic letter of John Paul II, *Ordinatio Sacerdotalis*, that outlaws priestly ordination for women and makes no mention of the diaconate. So, whether as "installed" (i.e., nonclerical) deacons, or as laypersons, women once again faced the iron gates of the Vatican barring their reentry to their historic ministry as deacons.

Without doubt, there is a concerted effort to bar women from the clerical state, because as clerics women could share power of governance. The objection of Benedict XVI to laypersons (and therefore all women) sharing power is concretized in canon 129, but this objection would be overtaken by diaconal ordination.

The enduring question is how (or even whether) to allow women to participate in governance and jurisdiction. The 1994 U.S. bishops' statement "Strengthening the Bonds of Peace" called only for women to consult and cooperate in the exercise of authority,[31] and refers to canon 129 of the 1983 Code of Canon Law, as presented earlier.[32] *Cooperate* is the key word, since an earlier term approved for this canon was *partem habere* ("participate"). Minority views supported different wording proposed by then Cardinal Joseph Ratzinger, and caused the change to *cooperare* ("cooperate").

Hence, the line was drawn by Benedict XVI, who in 1983 clearly wished to restrict governance and jurisdiction to clerics, and who will not consider the ordination of women to the priesthood.

Despite the fact that the ministering Church in South America, suffering a priest shortage prior to similar shortages in the United States and in Europe, presented its pastoral experience of women's ministry as a means of providing for the needs of the Church, the careful threads of Vatican statements and canon law remained and remain tightly woven against any incursion by women against the power and authority of governance. Laypersons cannot fully participate in governance, and women cannot be ordained to the clerical state.

The result is to bar participation in governance and jurisdiction by women (and other nonordained persons). But because the ordinary means by which persons enter the clerical state is through ordination to the diaconate, and because the Catholic Church has made no magisterial determination that this is impossible for women, there really is no legitimate reason why a diocesan bishop, in concert with the bishops of his province, could not restore the ancient tradition in his diocese if he and they deem it necessary. The Canon Law Society of America opined in 1995 that the nonadmission of women to the ancient office of deacon is a merely ecclesiastical law, one from which a derogation may be obtained.[33] The question becomes one of ecclesiology: Is a diocesan bishop the bishop of his particular church, or is he a "regional vice president," reporting to the one bishop of the West—the Patriarch of Rome—through his Curia?

The two most recent Vatican statements that touch on this question focus on the liceity and historicity of women deacons, but they do not form a definitive judgment relative to the possibilities for the future. The first statement, a 2001 notification on women deacons, indicated that women should not be trained for the diaconate. The second, the 2002 International Theological Commission document, concluded that women deacons of history do not equate to deacons today, but recognized that the actual determination on the ordination of women deacons is to be left to the magisterium.

The 2001 notification on the diaconal ordination of women, aimed mainly at the bishops of Germany, stated that "it is not licit to enact initiatives which, in some way, aim to prepare [women] candidates for diaconal ordination."[34] The notification argued that the preparation of women candidates for diaconal ordination was not licit because the Church does not envision it will ordain women to the diaconate. The four-sentence notification makes no comment on the conciliar canons of the fourth and fifth centuries relative to the ordination of women deacons, or other evidence of higher stature than the notification.

A year later, in 2002, the International Theological Commission published the seventy-two page document on the diaconate mentioned earlier, and which drew this conclusion:

> Regarding the ordination of women to the diaconate, it should be noted that two important points emerge from what has been set forth here: 1) the deaconesses mentioned in the ancient tradition of the Church—as suggested by their rite of institution and the functions

they exercised—are not purely and simply the same as deacons; 2) the unity of the sacrament of order, in the clear distinction between the ministries of the bishop and the priest on the one hand and the ministry of the deacon on the other, is strongly underscored by ecclesial tradition, above all in the doctrine of Vatican Council II and the postconciliar teaching of the Magisterium. In the light of these elements, supported by the evidence of the present historical-theological research, it will be up to the ministry of discernment, which the Lord has established in his Church, to speak authoritatively on this question.[35]

The document essentially re-presents the findings of the Council of Trent: the deacon is ordained not to the priesthood, but to the ministry. Its other finding, relative to the historical documentation of women deacons, skirts the evidence of their sacramental ordination.[36]

There have been no Vatican statements since 2002 on the restoration of the ancient tradition of women to the diaconate in the Catholic Church. The Orthodox Churches and the Oriental Orthodox Churches have begun to move back to the older tradition of women deacons. In the autocephalous Orthodox Church of Greece, only the monastic female diaconate is being restored, despite discussion in its Holy Synod of the need for a ministerial female diaconate. But in the Armenian Church, there are four ordained women deacons whose lives and ministry are fully engaged in the world around them, that is, who function as ministerial deacons.[37]

Even so, the ordained Armenian women deacons are all members of a religious order. There seem to be no formal efforts in the Orthodox or the Oriental Orthodox Churches to restore the female diaconate as a secular vocation, although women graduates of Orthodox theological schools, with the approbation of the Standing Conference of the Canonical Orthodox Bishops in the Americas,[38] have joined in an organization aimed at promoting women's ordained ministry. There are approximately two hundred Orthodox women seminary graduates in North America, most from Holy Cross Greek Orthodox School of Theology (Massachusetts) or St. Vladimir's Orthodox Theological School (New York).[39]

Given the apparent propensity in the Roman Catholic Church to look toward apostolic women religious to provide for diaconal ministry where no other solution is available, the further issue of ministry by women religious directed by a diocesan bishop arises. The incorporation of an individual into a society of apostolic life by no means automatically incurs ministerial credentials. In fact, it is an abuse of religious life to assert that such incorporation authorizes or requires any specific ministry without further training and certification.

Hence, several questions arise relative to the solution of the Venezuelan bishop noted above—that is, to use women religious as deacons in pastoral ministry—because the diaconal work of these women thereby becomes an extension of his episcopal office rather than an expression of the charism of their institute and its founders.[40] Women religious rightly chafe at the suggestion that their ministry be wholly under the control of the diocesan bishop, even though technically it is always so, independent of whether they belong to congregations or institutes of diocesan or papal right. This is because no official ministry can be undertaken in a diocese without the express permission of the diocesan bishop. The public ministry of women religious is more or less closely controlled, depending on individual ordinaries, but their ministry bears a strange resemblance to that of resigned and laicized priests, who often operate with the knowledge of, but without the delegated authority of, the diocesan bishop. In the case of women, authority cannot be delegated; in the case of resigned priests, it will not be delegated.[41] Each situation redounds to the stipulation of obedience to the diocesan bishop as a requirement for ministry within a territory. For the resigned and married priests, because of the irregularity of their commitment to celibacy, which was a condition of their ordination and remains a condition of their ability to function as Catholic priests, the diocesan bishop is actually unable to grant faculties.

The key to the power and authority of governance and jurisdiction in the Catholic Church is clearly marked "ordination." While some advocate abandonment of the entire system in the name of equality and of ministry, others argue for reform of the system as it stands. The operative question is: What will best serve the Church?

The waves of change after the Second Vatican Council opened the eyes, minds, and hearts of women and men to new-old possibilities for ministry, but may have raised false hopes as well. No one model can suffice for all the needs of the Church, but restoration of ancient practices seems within reach. The restoration of the female diaconate in the Catholic Church presents the possibility and the opportunity for diocesan ordinaries to add women to the permanent clergy of their dioceses, ministering perhaps much as apostolic women religious once did, and perhaps much as certified lay ministers now do. The difference is that these women, as ordained members of the clergy, would genuinely be able to share the power and authority of governance and jurisdiction, in a manner not seen in the Western Church in nearly 1,500 years.

CHAPTER TWO

CATHOLIC WOMEN'S ORDINATION

The Ecumenical Implications of Women Deacons in the Armenian Apostolic Church, the Orthodox Church of Greece, and Union of Utrecht Old Catholic Churches

The vexed question of the ordination of women in the Catholic Church[1] has widespread and deep implications for ecumenical dialogue between and among churches that ordain women, either to the diaconate, or to priesthood, or both. Three churches in dialogue with the Catholic Church—the Armenian Apostolic Church, the Orthodox Church of Greece, and certain Old Catholic Churches that are signers to the Union of Utrecht—are able to ordain women to the diaconate. While the Catholic Church recognizes the validity of sacraments and orders in these churches, it is unclear as to whether the validity of the ordination of women deacons in these churches would be equally recognized. There have been no Catholic statements regarding them.

The Armenian Apostolic Church has an unbroken tradition of ordaining monastic women deacons and today has women deacons in active ministries. The Orthodox Church of Greece is the most recent to join Churches whose apostolic succession is recognized by the Catholic Church and that ordain women. At least four Union of Utrecht Old Catholic Churches ordain women deacons and priests: the Old Catholic Churches in Germany (1996),[2] Austria (1998), the Netherlands (1998), and Switzerland (2002).[3] The Old Catholic Church in the Czech Republic ordained a woman deacon in 2003.

All of these ordinations are licit according to the requirements of their respective churches. These facts raise the question: does the Catholic Church also recognize these ordinations of women as valid? The restriction of orders at every level in the Catholic Church to males, rooted at the level of priesthood in the question of authority, is an ecclesial law not binding in these churches. Further, Catholic teaching does not necessarily hold that gender is a determinant of validity. Pius XII with the apostolic constitution *Sacramentum Ordinus* (1947) determined that "the only matter, of the Sacred Orders of the Diaconate, the Priesthood, and the Episcopacy, is the imposition of hands; and that the form, and the only form, is the words which determine the application of this matter...."[4] The gender of the ordinand is not part of the determination of matter or form. Assuming the ordinations in these churches are carried out with proper matter and form, then, it would seem that the ordinations are sacramentally valid as well as ecclesially licit within their respective churches. Given the older tradition of women deacons throughout Christianity, there seems no barrier to Rome's recognizing the validity of diaconal orders in these churches.[5]

To recognize the ecumenical implications of the ordination of women to the diaconate in these three churches in relation to the Catholic Church, the question must be necessarily split. The ordination of women to the diaconate is separate and distinct from the ordination of women to the priesthood. A major (yet flawed) argument against the ordination of women deacons in the Catholic Church is that such ordination would thereby qualify women for ordination to the priesthood: if you can ordain a woman deacon, then you can ordain a woman priest. However, there is nothing in custom or tradition to provide for the automatic entrance into the priesthood of an ordained deacon, male or female. Further, the Catholic Church has reasserted its tradition of a permanent diaconate in modern times.[6]

The opposing argument to ordaining Catholic women deacons also states that since the Catholic Church has definitively taught that a woman cannot be ordained a priest, so neither may she be ordained a deacon. Those who propose this argument overlook the fact that if the argument holds, then the reverse is also true: if women were ordained to the diaconate in the past, then they can be ordained in the present. That is, if the non-ordination of women deacons implies the impossibility of women priests, then the ordination of women deacons similarly implies the possibility of women priests. However, the Catholic Church has stated fairly clearly that it holds that women cannot be ordained priests. Hence, the ordination of women deacons in these three churches—or even in the Catholic Church— departs from neither custom nor tradition.

In addition, it seems obvious that conjoining the questions of women deacons and women priests serves neither side of the discussion. Those who ask for the restoration of the female diaconate are not necessarily asking for the ordination of women to the priesthood. Moreover, those who ask for ordination of women priests are not necessarily asking for ordination of women to the diaconate as a separate permanent ministry. The opposition to the ordination of women is equally ill served by conjoining the two, as demonstrated above. Arguing against ordained women deacons—who are an historical fact and a present reality in churches with whom the Catholic Church has common agreements—by stating that ordination to the diaconate implies the ability to ordain to the priesthood lends unintended support to the arguments for women deacons *and* for women priests.

It is important to recognize that the two modern documents about the ordination of women by the Catholic Church speak only to the ordination of women to the priesthood. The first, the Declaration of the Congregation for the Doctrine of the Faith *Inter Insigniores* (1976), presents both the "iconic argument" (Jesus must be represented by a male) and the "argument from authority" (Jesus chose only male apostles).[7] The second, the apostolic letter of John Paul II *Ordinatio Sacerdotalis* (1994), presents only the "argument from authority." It is addressed to the bishops of the Catholic Church and, as an apostolic letter, is not legislative in nature.[8] Further, the 1995 *Responsum ad Dubium* to questions surrounding the apostolic letter *Ordinatio Sacerdotalis* is an opinion rendered by the Congregation for the Doctrine of the Faith. While the opinion of infallibility rendered by the Congregation for the Doctrine of the Faith might seem to have more weight given the election of Benedict XVI, there is neither a *de jure divino* assertion of infallibility nor any clear papal statement relative to the infallibility of *Ordinatio Sacerdotalis*, which deals solely with priesthood and is based on the "argument from authority." Canonically, nothing is infallible unless it is clearly defined as such.[9] In any case, this second document on the ordination of women as priests does not address the question of women deacons.

The question of women deacons was taken up by multiple quinquennia of the International Theological Commission of the Congregation for the Doctrine of the Faith under the presidency of Cardinal Joseph Ratzinger, which concluded that the ordination of women deacons would require a decision of the magisterium, the full teaching office of the church.[10] Early ecumenical councils allow for the ordination of women to the diaconate (councils agreed to by all four churches in the present discussion),[11] but later local councils sought to curb the practice. Even so, in the Catholic Church as late as the eleventh century, the right to ordain women deacons was explicitly confirmed to a bishop in the West.[12] So there has been no modern ruling against the ordination of women deacons in the Catholic Church, and no ruling that overrides the conciliar documents or historic practice.[13]

Other documents of a higher order, specifically the Second Vatican Council document *Unitatis Redintegratio* (1964), speak directly to another point of this discussion. The Catholic Church recognizes several churches as having demonstrated apostolic succession, valid orders, and sacraments. The three churches named above—the Armenian Apostolic Church, which ordains women deacons; the Orthodox Church of Greece, which has voted to do so; and the Old Catholic Church of the Czech Republic, which has ordained a women deacon—along with four European member-churches of the Union of Utrecht that ordain women deacons and women priests (the Old Catholic Churches in Germany, Austria, the Netherlands, and Switzerland)—all have demonstrated such apostolic succession and valid orders. Prescinding from the fact of women priests in the four latter churches, each ordains women to the diaconate as well, which is the topic of this discussion.

It is well to examine the current situation in the three churches that find they can validly and licitly ordain women to the diaconate: the Armenian Apostolic Church, the Orthodox Church of Greece, and the Old Catholic Church of the Czech Republic.

THE ARMENIAN APOSTOLIC CHURCH

The history of the Armenian Apostolic Church, which traces its heritage to Saint Thaddeus and Saint Bartholomew, is somewhat confusing due to the fifteenth-century election of a catholicos in Echmiadzin, Armenia, the original seat of the church, while there was at the same time a catholicos in Cilicia, Lebanon, to which Armenians had fled in the tenth century. Since 1441, there have been two catholicosates in the Armenian Church with equal rights and privileges, and with their respective jurisdictions, although the primacy of honor of the Catholicosate of Echmiadzin has always been recognized by the Catholicosate of Cilicia. The See of Echmiadzin (Echmiadzin, Armenia) is led by His Holiness Karekin II, and the Armenian Catholicosate of Cilicia (Antelias, Lebanon) is led by His Holiness Aram I.

While the Armenian Apostolic Church is divided administratively into two separate and independent churches—Echmiadzin and Cilicia—the churches consider themselves to be one in the theological sense. The Catholic Church engages in dialogue with them separately within the context of dialogue with the Oriental Orthodox Churches. (The others in this dialogue are the Coptic Orthodox Patriarchate of Egypt; Syrian Orthodox Patriarchate of Antioch and All the East, Damascus; Orthodox Church of Ethiopia; Orthodox Church of Eritrea; and Malankara Syrian Orthodox Church.)

Without denying the hierarchical and juridical distinctions between and among these churches, and specifically between and among Echmiadzin and Cilicia and their adherents, the dialogue between the Catholic Church and the Oriental Orthodox Churches from the Catholic point of view must be understood within the context of the fundamental underlying conciliar document, *Unitatis Redintegratio*, which unequivocally recognizes the sacraments (and specifically Eucharist and orders) of the Oriental Orthodox Churches. In addition, there are three relatively recent joint or common declarations by the Catholic Church and the Armenian Church: that of May 12, 1970, between Paul VI and Vasken I, Supreme Catholicos and Patriarch of all Armenians (Echmiadzin, 1955–95); of December 13, 1996, between John Paul II and His Holiness Karekin I, Supreme Patriarch and Catholicos of All Armenians (Echmiadzin, 1995–99); and of January 25, 1997, between Pope John Paul II and Catholicos Aram I Keshishian (Cilicia, 1995–present).

The Armenian Apostolic Church has a modern history of monastic women deacons who served as deacons during the Divine Liturgy in their convents and who, since the mid-twentieth century, have served as deacons in the liturgy in parish churches and cathedrals (in Echmiadzin, Tiflis, and Constantinople). The Armenian Catholicosate of Cilicia has at least three ordained women in Lebanon, and the Armenian Patriarchate of Constantinople lists at least one protodeacon, Mother Hrip'sime, who was ordained in 1984.[14] Her name is that of the legendary virgin who fled the advances of the Emperor Diocletian to Armenia, where she refused King Tiridates, who had her and her companions tortured and killed. Many women servants of the Armenian Church have taken her name; there are extant photographs of nineteenth-century protodeacon Sister Hrip'sime Aghek'-Tahireanc' of Jerusalem in her liturgical vestments.[15]

The Diocese of the Armenian Church in America (East) has recently begun to call its historical women deacons "deaconesses," distinguishing the "deaconess" (a monastic woman deacon) from a "woman deacon" (an active woman deacon not in a religious order). Even so, the Armenian Apostolic Church considers these women to be truly ordained. Since the Armenian Apostolic Church is interested in its relations with Catholics, Orthodox, other Oriental Orthodox, and Anglicans, recognition of the validity of the orders of ordained women—its own and those of other churches— and the validity of the sacraments they perform is extremely important.

The ordination of women deacons is not a point of division between the Armenian Church and the Anglican, Orthodox, or Oriental Orthodox Churches, but it does raise questions in ecumenical dialogue between it and the Catholic Church, which has not responded to these apparently valid and licit ordinations.

THE ORTHODOX CHURCH OF GREECE

The vote of the Holy Synod of the autocephalous Orthodox Church of Greece in October 2004 to restore the female diaconate marks an important return to tradition by this branch of Orthodoxy. Even though it did not have to take the matter to a vote—three ecumenical councils honored by the Orthodox have already determined that women can be ordained to the diaconate—the Church's entire Holy Synod considered the topic.[16] Their decision does not affect the Greek Orthodox Archdiocese of America or the Greek

Orthodox Church as it exists in Australia, Canada, Ireland, the United Kingdom, or other parts of the world, each of which is part of the Ecumenical Patriarchate headquartered in Constantinople and led by the Ecumenical Patriarch Bartholomew I. The Orthodox Church of Greece declared its autocephaly unilaterally in 1833 and received its independence from Constantinople in 1850.[17]

The Joint International Commission for Theological Dialogue between the Catholic Church and the Orthodox Church was created on the occasion of the visit of Pope John Paul II to the Ecumenical Patriarchate in 1979. During its fifth plenary session in 1988, in which the fourteen autocephalous and autonomous Orthodox Churches (including the Orthodox Church of Greece) took part, the commission approved "The Sacrament of Order in the Sacramental Structure of the Church, with Particular Reference to the Importance of the Apostolic Succession for the Sanctification and Unity of the People of God." This document depends upon the common affirmation of the apostolic succession and validity of sacraments of each member of the commission ("We rely on the certitude that in our Churches apostolic succession is fundamental for the sanctification and the unity of the people of God"),[18] but the document leaves the matter of papal primacy for further meetings.

The document defines the diaconate as part of the sacrament of order, "exercised at the service of the bishop and the priest, in the liturgy, in the work of evangelization and in the service of charity."[19] It leaves the discussion of the diaconate at that. It does not directly address women deacons. The document appeals to tradition regarding the ordination of women to priesthood:

Throughout the entire history of our Churches, women have played a fundamental role, as witnessed not only by the most Holy Mother of God, but also by the holy women mentioned in the New Testament, by the numerous women saints whom we venerate, as well as by so many other women who up to the present day have served the Church in many ways. Their particular charisms are very important for the building up of the Body of Christ. But our Churches remain faithful to the historical and theological tradition according to which they ordain only men to the priestly ministry. (No. 32)

The document's following paragraph appears to reaffirm the "iconic argument" against the ordination of women:

Just as the apostles gathered together the first communities, by proclaiming Christ, by celebration [sic] the eucharist, by leading the baptised towards growing communion with Christ and with each other, so the bishop, established by the same Spirit, continues to preach the same Gospel, to preside at the same eucharist, to serve the unity and sanctification of the same community. He is thus the icon of Christ the servant among his brethren. (No. 33)

However, while the joint Catholic-Orthodox document makes no connection, explicit or implicit, between the diaconate and the priesthood or the episcopate, the notion of "Christ the servant" is more in keeping with the theology of the diaconate. Even so, there is no discrepancy between the deacon and bishop, each being the "icon of Christ the servant," since the episcopacy incorporates the diaconate as well as the priesthood. (In modern times the Catholic priesthood incorporates the diaconate as well, but not to such a degree that the priest as icon of "Christ...Bridegroom and

Head of the Church"[20] cannot concurrently be deacon and "icon of Christ the servant.") That is, any "iconic argument" rendered can be distinguished between an "iconic argument" on behalf of priesthood and an "iconic argument" on behalf of the diaconate, necessarily conjoined in the episcopacy (and there symbolized by the bishops' wearing of both a priestly chasuble and a diaconal dalmatic in major ceremonies, especially ordinations).[21]

This governing document relative to the Catholic Church's understanding of the apostolic succession and validity of orders of the Orthodox Church of Greece—and of all Orthodoxy—makes no statement regarding the long-standing tradition of Orthodox women deacons, ordained in modern times according to the ancient Byzantine ritual used by Orthodox Saint Nectarious (1846–1920), bishop of Pentapolis, who ordained two women deacons in 1911.[22] Up to the 1950s, Greek Orthodox nuns became monastic deaconesses, and in 1986, Christodoulos, then metropolitan of Demetrias and now the archbishop of Athens and all of Greece, ordained a woman deacon according to the same ritual. Archbishop Christodoulos presided over the October 2004 Synod that voted to restore the practice of monastic women deacons throughout the Church of Greece, although some Synod members asked for ordained women deacons active in social ministry as well.[23] It is generally understood that "ordination" *(cheirotonia)* is envisioned, as opposed to "blessing" *(cheirothesia)*.[24]

Like the ordination of women deacons in the Armenian Church, the ordination of women deacons in Orthodoxy poses questions only for the Catholic Church in ecumenical dialogue with its sister churches.

OLD CATHOLIC CHURCHES

In 1889, Old Catholic bishops of the Netherlands, Austria, Germany, and Switzerland signed the Union of Utrecht. The Church of Utrecht was formed in the Netherlands in late 1723 in reaction to papal assertion of authority over the Netherlands' clergy and property. In 1870, Old Catholic dioceses were established by the Union of Utrecht in response to the dogmas of papal infallibility and supreme jurisdiction of Vatican I. The Union of Utrecht also rejects the dogma of the Immaculate Conception promulgated by Pius IX in 1854 and rejects the disciplines (but not the doctrine) of the Council of Trent.

Today, member churches of the Union of Utrecht of the Old Catholic Churches are represented in the International Old Catholic Bishops' Conference, whose ex officio head is the Old Catholic Archbishop of Utrecht. The member Churches—the Old Catholic Church of the Netherlands, Catholic Diocese of the Old Catholics in Germany, Old Catholic Church of Austria, Christian Catholic Church of Switzerland, Old Catholic Church of the Czech Republic, and the Polish Catholic Church of Poland—are considered by the Catholic Church to have valid sacraments and orders. The Polish National Catholic Church in the United States (Scranton, Pennsylvania), which the Catholic Church also considers to have valid sacraments, does not ordain women and no longer belongs to the Union of Utrecht.[25]

Those in full communion with Union of Utrecht Old Catholics are the Anglican Communion and the Philippine Independent Church.[26] There are numerous Old Catholic groups in the United States, some of which claim to be descendants of Union of Utrecht Old Catholic Churches.[27] While the Catholic Church technically regards their orders

Catholic Women's Ordination

and sacraments as valid, when the clergy of these various Old Catholic groups in the United States request reception to the Catholic Church, they are received as laypersons.

For the purposes of this essay, the focus is on the Old Catholic Churches signers to the Union of Utrecht that the Catholic Church recognizes as having valid sacraments and orders.

The votes of the synods of the Old Catholic Churches in Germany, Austria, the Netherlands, and Switzerland to admit women to the diaconate and, later, to the priesthood and, in theory, to the episcopate led the Old Catholic Church in the Czech Republic to consider the matter. At its 2003 Synod, the Old Catholic Church in the Czech Republic failed to approve a proposal to open all grades of order to women. However, the proposal to admit women to the diaconate was accepted by vote (27 yes, 3 no, 16 abstentions). At that time there was only one female candidate for the diaconate and none for other grades of order. Hana Karasova was ordained deacon in October 2003 by Old Catholic Bishop Dusan Hejbal.[28] The next synod to be convened by the Old Catholic Church in the Czech Republic may take up the matter of women priests. In the meanwhile, the Old Catholic Church in the Czech Republic is the only Western Church whose orders and apostolic succession are recognized by the Catholic Church that ordains women solely to the diaconate and, affirmatively, not to priesthood.

Prescinding from the practices of other Old Catholic Churches, and assuming the apostolic succession of the ordaining Czech Old Catholic bishop, the ordination of Hana Karasova creates a window to the West independent of, and not to be confused with, the late twentieth-century ordinations of women deacons and priests in the underground Catholic Church in the Czech Republic.[29]

CONCLUSION

The Catholic Church has made a limited attempt to deny the history and possibility of women deacons through various curial statements, as well as with the 2002 document of the International Theological Commission, "*Le Diaconate: Évolution et Perspectives*," which argues that the rite of institution and functions of the women deacons of the ancient Church were not identical to those of the men deacons of the ancient church.[30] Yet, in churches that have not fully abandoned the tradition (which happened around the sixth century in the West and, for the most part, the eleventh century in the East, until modern times) women have been and are being ordained to the diaconate. The likely ritual for the Orthodox Church of Greece is derived from the *Apostolic Constitutions*[31] and comprises a ritual deep in the history of the Catholic Church as well.

For a church recognized as having valid orders by the Catholic Church to use this ritual in modern times with the authority of tradition brings forth multiple questions regarding interchurch relations and could move forward the internal discussion of restoring the tradition of women deacons in the Catholic Church. This is especially true in the cases of the three churches discussed here.

The ecumenical dimension of the female diaconate cannot be ignored. Clearly, should a Catholic curial office declare the orders of women deacons in the Armenian Apostolic Church, Orthodox Church of Greece, and/or Old Catholic Churches invalid, such could force a serious fracture in ecumenical relations. The Catholic reaction to the ordination of women priests (but not women deacons) in Anglicanism sets precedence for a reaction, but not for a reaction regarding women deacons.[32] (The Catholic reaction to the ordination of

Anglican women is curious in light of the encyclical of Leo XIII, *Apostolicae Curae* [September 18, 1896], which declares Anglican orders null. If Anglican orders are null, why would it matter if Anglican women are ordained?) Even so, the Catholic Church has made no official comment on the ordination of women deacons in Anglicanism.

Despite discussion of the question of monastic or non-monastic women deacons, the Orthodox and Oriental Orthodox Churches apparently do not consider the orders of their women deacons the equivalent of minor orders. So also do the Union of Utrecht Old Catholic Churches clearly consider their ordination of women to the diaconate as ordination to major orders. However, even without consideration of the actions taken by the Old Catholic Church in the Czech Republic, or those Old Catholic Churches in Switzerland, Germany, Austria, and the Netherlands, official Catholic reaction to the ordination of women to the diaconate in the Orthodox and Oriental Orthodox Churches would shed light on the Catholic Church's understanding of its own history.

Independent of whether the ordained women of the Orthodox and Oriental Orthodox Churches have been or are to be ordained as monastic women deacons to serve only within their monasteries, or as women deacons in service to the larger community, their churches recognize them as validly ordained to major orders; the Catholic Church's response can solidify or explode the ecumenical balance between and among the various churches involved. Granted, other issues divide Christianity with equal energy and emotion, but none has such clear support of the ancient tradition of the Church.[33]

Prescinding from the fact of priestly ordinations in some of the Union of Utrecht Old Catholic Churches and other Christian denominations, there remain few Christian denominations that do not ordain women deacons. If the Catholic Church chose to recognize and return to the larger and longer tradition of ordaining women deacons, it might solidify its position on the ordination of women priests. As noted above, the Catholic Church argues that it does not have the authority to ordain women to the priesthood. If that argument is correct, the Catholic Church could easily return to the tradition of ordaining women deacons. If that argument is not correct, then the delay in a return to the tradition is political rather than theological.

It would seem logical that a decision by the Catholic Church to return to its tradition of ordaining women deacons might better foster Christian unity, as well as help the Catholic Church regain its lost authority in matters of human rights and equality.

Without question, the ordination of women deacons is one of singular interest and import in ecumenical discussion. Prior to the election of Benedict XVI, Cardinal Walter Kasper, president of the Pontifical Council for Promoting Christian Unity (and a member of the Congregations for the Doctrine of the Faith and for Eastern Churches), told a reporter in New York that the question of ordaining women to the diaconate is "not settled."[34] His comment could be read as recognition of apparent unwillingness or inability of the requisite dicasteries to render a decision, but the fact that he commented on the record at all supports the import of the topic.

The reasons given for the continued refusal to render a decision on restoring the female diaconate obliquely (and perhaps unintentionally) present the Catholic Church's need for ministry by women deacons. In the same meeting, Cardinal Kasper added that women were already doing what they would do if they were ordained as deacons.[35] Such is not the case. While by exceptional rescripts women sometimes can fulfill some duties of deacons (witnessing marriages, solemnly baptizing), there are canonical restrictions against laypersons preaching or sharing authority. The Code of Canon Law (as well as the Code of Canons of the Eastern Churches) specifically forbids nonordained persons to preach at eucharistic liturgies or have any ordinary juridical authority.[36] For example, a woman may be a member of a marriage tribunal, but as a noncleric she cannot be a single signer of an opinion. Such would evidence ordinary juridical authority of a woman over a man. Similarly, the neuralgic issues of preaching and functioning in diaconal capacity at liturgy, particularly at the Liturgy of the Eucharist, are expressly forbidden. Each flares at the prospect of ordained women deacons in the Catholic Church.

Hence, while a number of diaconal ministries are performed by nonordained persons, and certain diaconal juridical and sacramental authority can be delegated to nonordained persons, no Catholic woman genuinely functions as a deacon.

The 2002 International Theological Commission document states that the functions of women deacons of the ancient Church are not the same as the functions of the deacon today.[37] Still, the document makes no clear statement about whether women were sacramentally ordained, or whether the tradition will be revived. What the Church has done, the Church can do again. Women are ordained in churches whose sacraments and apostolic succession are recognized by the Catholic Church. How, exactly, does the Catholic Church view them? If the Catholic Church recognizes their unbroken or returned-to tradition, will it recognize its own?

These questions need to be asked. And these questions need to be answered.

CHAPTER THREE

THE QUESTION OF GOVERNANCE AND MINISTRY FOR WOMEN[1]

When Father Mark Valentini, on March 2, 2006, rose to ask his bishop a question, he may not have expected the answer he received. The thirty-nine-year-old priest told his bishop, and the other assembled priests of his diocese, that he had recent and positive experience of the ministry of women—both married and religious—to priests in crisis. It set him to thinking, he said: Why not put women side by side with men in the governance of the Church? Every Church decision is taken from the male point of view, Father Valentini continued, but women work at the charismatic level through prayer and at the practical level as well. Recall, he said, how Catherine of Siena brought the pope back to Rome. Perhaps, Valentini continued, women's point of view at the institutional level could help not only priests in difficulty, but all priests in decision making.

More simply put: Why not include women in the ministry and governance of the Church?

This little story is perhaps not unusual. Priests and deacons around the world have been speaking with their parishioners and among themselves, and they have been asking their bishops this very question: Why is it that women cannot have a greater role in the governance and ministry of the Church? It is a worldwide question, but the difference in this particular case is that the priest who asked it, Father Mark Valentini, is a parochial vicar of the Church of San Girolamo a Corviale, in Rome; his bishop is Pope Benedict XVI.[2]

The format of the meeting Valentini attended on March 2, 2006—the pope's traditional meeting with the priests in his diocese at the beginning of Lent—allowed fifteen priests to present questions that Benedict then answered one by one. Valentini's question stood out among them, as he stood out among the people and the priests of Rome. There are 2.8 million people, 335 parishes, and over 5,000 priests in the diocese of Rome. Whatever lottery allowed Valentini even to ask his question is only slightly short of miraculous.

Pope Benedict answered another young priest's question just before he addressed Valentini's. After commenting on the priest's youth—at seventy-nine the pope was more than twice Father Valentini's age—Benedict responded at length. His response includes two key concepts: "governance" and "ministry":

> In response to the assistant pastor of San Girolamo—
> I see that he too is very young—who spoke about how much women do in the church, also on behalf of priests. I am only able to underscore how the special prayer for priests in the first Canon, the Roman Canon, always makes a great impression on me. "*Nobis quoque peccatoribus.*" In this realistic humility of us priests, precisely as sinners, we pray that the Lord will help us to be his servants. In this prayer of the priest, and only in it, seven women appear who surround him.[3] They demonstrate how women believers help us on our way. Certainly everyone of us has this experience. Thus, the

Church owes an enormous debt of gratitude to women. And you have correctly emphasized that, at a charismatic level, women do so much, I would dare say, for the governance of the Church, beginning with the sisters of the great Fathers of the Church,[4] such as Saint Ambrose, to the great women of the Middle Ages—Saint Hildegard, Saint Catherine of Siena, then Saint Teresa of Avila—up to Mother Teresa. I would say this charismatic work certainly is distinct from ministry in the strict sense of the word, but it is a genuine and deep participation in the governance of the Church. How is it possible to imagine the governance of the Church without this contribution, which sometimes becomes very visible, as when Saint Hildegard criticized the bishops, or when Saint Brigid and Saint Catherine of Siena admonished and obtained the return of the Popes to Rome? It [the contribution of women] is always a crucial factor, without which the Church cannot live. However, you rightly say: we want to see even more clearly, in a ministerial way, women in the governance of the Church. I would say this is precisely the question. The priestly ministry from the Lord is, as we know, reserved to men, inasmuch as priestly ministry is governance in the profound sense that, in fact, it is the Sacrament that governs the Church. This is the decisive point. It is not the man who does something, but the priest faithful to his mission who governs, in the sense that it is the Sacrament, that is, through the Sacrament it is Christ himself who governs [:] whether through the Eucharist or the other sacraments, it is always Christ who presides. However, it is proper to ask whether in this ministerial service—notwithstanding the fact that here Sacrament and charism are one and the same track (*binario*) on which the Church realizes itself—it is not possible to offer more space, more positions of responsibility to women.[5]

These four hundred off-the-cuff words in the original Italian, as transcribed by the Zenit News Agency and published on the Vatican Web site,[6] are Benedict's first direct comments on the matter. Yet, the length and depth of his reply indicates the energy surrounding the simple question he repeated: Why not have women in ministry and governance?

Why not? Benedict repeated his partial litany of women who have served the Church: Hildegard, Catherine of Siena, Teresa of Avila, and Mother Teresa. Their service was indeed ministry in the broader sense, but when speaking to the future for women, Benedict more likely used the word *ministry* in its technical sense. So, too, with *governance*. Since the usual path to governance and ministry in the Catholic Church is by ordination, Benedict's apparent agreement that women can, or at least should, have greater share in governance and ministry is surprising.

What is not surprising is his restatement of the objections to the ordination of women to priesthood. However, even prescinding from ordination to priesthood, the pope still allowed that there might be more "space" for women: "più spazio, più posizioni di responsabilità alle donne." That is, he asked: Why not allow women to minister and share governance in the Church?

The terms under discussion that day are clearly *ministry* and *governance*. Technically speaking, each requires ordination, but not necessarily priestly ordination.

GOVERNANCE

"Governance" has a particular meaning in canon law and in theology. Generally speaking, the "power of governance" is vested by the Church in the clergy. However, among what are called the "triple *munera*" or the "triple offices" of the Church—the teaching office, the sanctifying office, and the governing office—there is no section in canon law specifically directed at the governing office of the Church, or governance.

The section in canon law that considers governance is "*de potestate regiminis*" ("on the power of governance"). This terminology does not correspond to the terminology of Vatican II, which speaks to "the power of jurisdiction" or, simply, "jurisdiction." Neither does the section on the power of governance speak to the governing office.

Canon law clearly holds that women cannot *participate* in governance, although women may consult and cooperate in it. In 1994, the bishops of the United States issued a statement entitled "Strengthening the Bonds of Peace," in which they wrote: "An important issue for women is how to have a voice in the governance of the Church to which they belong and which they serve with love and generosity. This can be achieved in at least two ways that are consistent with church teaching: through consultation and through cooperation in the exercise of authority."[7] The key words here are *consultation* and *cooperation* in the exercise of authority. Neither implies authority, or power, or jurisdiction, or governance for the laity. Hence, neither implies authority, or power, or jurisdiction, or governance for women—all of whom are laypersons—in the Church at large.

A footnote to this passage reiterated the provisions of canon 129 of the 1983 Code of Canon Law, which states who can exercise the power of governance:

1. Those who have received sacred orders are qualified, according to the norm of the prescripts of the law, for

the power of governance, which exists in the Church by divine institution and is also called the power of jurisdiction.

2. Lay members of the Christian faithful can cooperate in the exercise of this same power according to the norm of law.

Valentini's question was about women in the governance of the Church, and Benedict replied: "You rightly say: 'we want to see even more visibly, in a ministerial way, women in the governance of the church.' I would say this is exactly the question."[8]

The organizational relationships of the Church are described by canon law. Canon 129 and the question of who can exercise the power of governance is critical to the present discussion, because the operative word in this canon, relative to the laity and the power of governance, is *cooperate*. Laity—and all women are laypersons—can *cooperate* in governance, but only the ordained can hold the power of governance.[9]

It is well to recall that the 1983 revision of the 1917 Code of Canon Law found two competing schools of canonists considering what came to be canon 129. The text of canon 129 in the 1981 *Plenaria* on proposed revisions to the Code was this: "Lay members of the Christian faithful can participate in the exercise of this same power according to the norm of law." That is, a draft of the canon allowed laypersons to "participate" (*partem habere*). But, of the two schools of thought, the "Roman" school gave way to the more conservative wording of the "Munich" school, which was proposed by then Cardinal Joseph Ratzinger. So *participate* was replaced by *cooperate*.[10] The language proposed by Cardinal Ratzinger and accepted by the *Plenaria,* and now in the Code of Canon Law, however, is the same as the language Pope Benedict used on March 2, 2006, referring to the possible role of women in the Church.

The pope does not intend to ordain women priests and bishops, but he clearly spoke to the possibility of governance and ministry for women. While governance and ministry are presently restricted to the clergy, Benedict answered that both might be possible for women.

WOMEN DEACONS

The only way Benedict can technically include women in formal governance and ministry is by restoring women to the ordained diaconate, which he has both the power and authority to do. Two ecumenical councils agreed to by all Christendom—Nicaea (325) and Chalcedon (451)—speak to the ordination of women to the diaconate.[11] Canon 19 of the Council of Nicaea describes the Paulianist women ministers as deaconesses, but counts them among the laity because they did not receive the laying on of hands, and says they must be both rebaptized and reordained.[12] Canon 15 of the Council of Chalcedon assumes the ordination of deaconesses and lowered the allowable age of ordination candidates from sixty to forty: "A woman shall not be ordained as a deaconess below the age of forty."[13]

Some local councils restricted what apparently continued for some time as the common practice of ordaining women deacons. Copious published research presents epigraphical, literary, and liturgical evidence of this tradition continuing even to the eleventh century in both East and West, such that the fact of women deacons is not a historical unknown.[14]

The power of the Church to call women to diaconal

orders has been recently contested, but this contention does not override the prior determinations of councils. As late as the eleventh century, the right of a diocesan ordinary to ordain women deacons was confirmed, as in the 1017 letter of Pope Benedict VIII to the bishop of Porto in Portugal, which confirms that diocesan ordinary's privileges: "We concede and confirm to you and to your successors in perpetuity every episcopal ordination (*ordinationem episcopalem*), not only of presbyters but also of deacons or deaconesses (*diaconissis*) or subdeacons."[15] That is, the episcopal right of a diocesan ordinary to ordain (not "appoint" or "bless") women deacons in his own diocese was confirmed by a pope. The fact that women deacons or deaconesses are listed ahead of subdeacons supports the notion that they were ordained to major orders.

The East presents even more recent evidence. In addition to the deep history regarding women deacons in the West, some churches in "imperfect communion" with the Catholic Church—some Orthodox and Oriental Orthodox Churches—never wholly abandoned the practice of ordaining women deacons, at least monastic women deacons.[16] They generally continued the practice well into the sixteenth century and, in some places, into the nineteenth century.

In our century, the Holy Synod of the Orthodox Church of Greece voted in October 2004 to restore women's monastic diaconate, specifically to assist in the liturgy and to minister to ill sisters. But some Synod members asked about a nonmonastic ministerial female diaconate as well, to provide for needs outside the monastery.[17]

The Catholic Church and the Armenian Apostolic Church recognize each other's sacraments and apostolic succession. The Armenian Apostolic Church already ordains women deacons, at least three of whom belong to a religious order and run an orphanage in Lebanon.[18]

These Churches, the Orthodox Church of Greece and the Armenian Apostolic Church, speak to Benedict's suggestion that women can be more fully incorporated into the (ordained) ministry of the Catholic Church. The synod fathers of the Orthodox Church of Greece asked for active women deacons, and the ordained women deacons of the Armenian Apostolic Church already live the active charism of "ministry" to the people of God in the technical sense Benedict refers to.

THE PROBLEM OF HISTORY

The problem of history arises in considering women in governance and ministry in the contemporary Catholic Church, particularly in the Latin Church. The Eastern Churches mentioned above are in what the Catholic Church calls "imperfect communion" with it. Yet, given that these Eastern Churches have common history with the Catholic Church and, based on that history, are ordaining women in their traditions, it would seem that the Catholic Church can do the same. That is, these churches look back to the same Scripture, the same history, the same liturgies, and the same historical materials that the Catholic Church does, and they ordain or say they will ordain women deacons. But common history and ancestry have not been persuasive, at least in the Catholic Church.

There has been some contemporary discussion and a few official documents regarding the restoration of the female diaconate in the Catholic Church. A September 2001 notification on the diaconal ordination of women from the

Congregation for the Doctrine of the Faith, the Congregation for Divine Worship and the Discipline of the Sacraments, and the Congregation for Clergy directed at the bishops of Germany stated that "it is not licit to enact initiatives which, in some way, aim to prepare [women] candidates for diaconal ordination."[19] In essence, the notification argued that women should not be prepared for diaconal ordination because the signers to the notification did not wish to ordain women to the diaconate. It made no doctrinal determination.

The notification was followed in 2002 by a seventy-two-page document on the diaconate published by the International Theological Commission (ITC) of the Congregation for the Doctrine of the Faith (CDF) when both were headed by Cardinal Joseph Ratzinger. As such, the 2002 ITC document is the highest-level, contemporary, official document that addresses the question of women deacons. Entitled "Le Diaconat: Évolution et perspectives" and officially published only in French, the document actually left open the possibility of the restoration of the female diaconate in the Catholic Church. One point of consideration within the document was history: how to interpret the historical evidence for women deacons. Perhaps predictably, the ITC did not interpret the evidence of women deacons of history in the most positive light. The ITC's exact words are:

> Regarding the ordination of women to the diaconate, it should be noted that two important points emerge from what has been set forth here: 1) The deaconesses mentioned in the ancient tradition of the Church—as suggested by their rite of institution and the functions they exercised—are not purely and simply the same as deacons; 2) The unity of the sacrament of order, in the

clear distinction between the ministries of the bishop and the priest on the one hand and the ministry of the deacon on the other, is strongly underscored by ecclesial tradition, above all in the doctrine of Vatican Council II and the postconciliar teaching of the Magisterium. In the light of these elements, supported by the evidence of the present historical-theological research, it will be up to the ministry of discernment, which the Lord has established in his Church, to speak authoritatively on this question.[20]

The ITC, therefore, concluded that (1) its interpretation of history does not support a historical argument for women deacons; (2) the sacrament of order clearly distinguishes between the ministries of the bishop and priest and those of the deacon; and (3) the "ministry of discernment"—essentially the magisterium—will have to make the decision on women deacons. How long it will take for "the ministry of discernment, which the Lord has established in his Church, to speak authoritatively" on women deacons is unclear, especially since it appears that the ordinary magisterium (Pope Benedict VIII) and the extraordinary magisterium (Councils of Nicaea and Chalcedon) have already made determinations, each within the *consensus fidelium*. If the churches in "imperfect communion" (the Orthodox Church of Greece and the Armenian Apostolic Church) are added to the mix, then their bishops, too, might be seen—at least in theory—to contribute to the ordinary universal magisterium, in concert with the Latin bishops who have called for women deacons, including the late Cardinal Basil Hume,[21] Cardinal Carlo Maria Martini,[22] and Bishop Roger J. Vangheluwe of Bruges.[23] Further, Bartholomew, Ecumenical Patriarch of Constantinople, has confirmed the possibility of returning to the "ancient tradition of the Church" of ordaining women to the diaconate.[24]

While the question as examined by the ITC was first returned to John Paul II for definitive pronouncement, it now rests with Benedict XVI.

The ITC's first objection rests in the interpretation of history. Benedict knows well the pitfalls of history and the illusion of objectivity. In 1988, when, as prefect of the CDF, Benedict spoke in St. Peter's Lutheran Church in New York City, he said that the attempt of the historical-critical method to instill scientific precision on scriptural exegesis calls itself into question as shown by the Heisenberg Uncertainty Principle:[25]

> Now, if the natural science model is to be followed without hesitation, then the importance of the Heisenberg principle should be applied to the historical-critical method as well. Heisenberg has shown that the outcome of a given experiment is heavily influenced by the point of view of the observer. So much is this the case that both observer's questions and observations continue to change themselves in the natural course of events. When applied to the witness of history, this means that interpretation can never be just a simple reproduction of history's being, "as it was." The word *interpretation* gives us a clue to the question itself: every exegesis requires an "inter"—an entering in and a being "inter," or between things; this is the involvement of the interpreter himself. Pure objectivity is an absurd abstraction. It is not the uninvolved who comes to knowledge; rather, interest itself is a requirement for the possibility of coming to know.[26]

While Benedict's 1988 lecture was directed at excesses of the historical-critical method of scriptural exegesis, the question of objectivity applies to the question of women deacons as well. If, as Benedict posits, "pure objectivity is an absurd abstraction," then the historical premise of the ITC document, even if true, does not hold. For, as Valentini might remind us, the history of women deacons in the ITC document is read through the lens of the ITC's (all male) drafting committee.

History is not normative in either direction relative to the restoration of the female diaconate, for it is impossible to create an essentially revisionist history and impose it on current theology. Hence, independent of disputed interpretations, history alone cannot determine the essential question regarding women deacons: Is there a need for the restoration of the female diaconate in the Church today? The real question is "ministry," as it is most narrowly defined, and the needs of the Church.

MINISTRY

It is most important not to confuse ecclesial ministries with states of life within the Church. States of life are particular ways of living the Christian life, and in the Catholic Church all persons are either seculars or religious. Within each category, secular and religious, there are both clerics and laypersons. So individuals might be secular clerics or secular laypersons, or religious clerics or religious laypersons. Individuals of each of these descriptors may also participate in various Church ministries. In the ordained ministries of bishop, priest, or deacon, there are both secular and religious clerics. In the nonordained ministries of acolyte, lector, and lay ecclesial minister, there are also both secular and religious laypersons. This discussion centers on the entrance of both women religious and laywomen to the clerical state, and on the need for ordained female diaconal ministry.

Permanent deacons, who may be seculars or religious, are foremost the ministers of charity. Benedict's response to Valentini, read in light of his emphasis on the works of charity—the charismatic ministry—as the heart of the Church's mission, points the whole Church in the direction of the diaconate. In his first encyclical, *Deus Caritas Est* ("God Is Love"),[27] a 15,000-word, carefully crafted discourse on the root, nature, and function of Christian love, from the personal and interpersonal to the institutional levels, Benedict clearly stated that the works of charity are at the heart of the Church's function.

Benedict spoke directly of the ministry of charity in part 2 of the encyclical, where he made it quite clear that responsibility for the ministry of charity in a particular church rests with the diocesan ordinary. He cited the rite of episcopal ordination,[28] canon law, and the new *Directory for the Pastoral Ministry of Bishops* in support of his point. Benedict quotes the *Directory*: "The duty of charity [is] a responsibility incumbent upon the whole Church and upon each Bishop in his Diocese."[29]

Two related concepts cannot be overlooked: (1) the freedom and duty of a diocesan ordinary to act in his diocese, and (2) the ministries of charity carried out by women worldwide. The link is inescapable. If a bishop wishes to expand the works of charity in his diocese, he has an expert and experienced cadre of persons willing to minister—in the technical sense of the word—to the poor and the needy and the sick and the imprisoned. In fact, these persons are already living the *kenosis* that diaconal work requires. They are in all likelihood as prepared for ordination as any or are willing to be prepared, but they are women.[30] At least in the past two hundred years, and until very recently, the preponderance of the women serving in nonordained diaconal roles in ecclesial structures, particularly in the parishes, have been apostolic religious, whose numbers and service in developed countries are presently eclipsed by those of secular women lay ecclesial ministers. As of 2005, of the approximately 30,000 paid lay ecclesial ministers in the United States, 64 percent are secular women, 16 percent are women religious, and 20 percent are secular and religious men.[31] In short, 80 percent of the lay ecclesial ministers in the United States are women. There are no studies that specifically track how many of these are wives of deacons and so may have already completed diaconal training alongside their husbands. Given the general decline of apostolic communities of women religious—at least in developed countries—the question of whether women religious would wish to be ordained is effectively moot, although the development of an institute of women religious that is either mixed lay and clerical (i.e., *including* women deacons) or wholly clerical (i.e., *only* women deacons) is quite conceivable.[32]

Whether the female diaconate would best be initially revived within religious institutes, as in the Armenian Apostolic Church and the Orthodox Church of Greece, or as an ordained vocation open to all women, secular and religious, is hard to determine. Since deacons are mostly unpaid part-time ministers, women deacons would have to find a means for subsistence, whether by full-time ecclesial, private, or secular employment, by personal retirement funds, or by membership in a religious institute or order. In this last case, the institute or order would expect their religious deacon to work full-time either for the diocese or parish, or in a ministry of the institute or order. Other than at schools, orphanages, and hospitals, this latter option might mirror the situation of permanent deacons who today are employed in other than diocesan or parochial ministry, and who exercise their liturgical ministries in locales separate from their places of employment, typically in their own or nearby parishes as assigned by their bishops.

Even so, it is reasonable to surmise that, given Benedict's understanding of the current situation in the Church and in the world, he might choose to ordain women deacons sooner rather than later. The ancient order need not be restored worldwide immediately. Rather, it is possible that individual bishops could—and possibly should—restore it in their individual dioceses as need arises.

Individual bishops could look to women deacons precisely because the bishop's responsibility, as Benedict reminded them, is to charity. It appears that individual bishops could revive the order, given that ecumenical councils and popes have confirmed the ability of bishops to ordain women deacons. No higher authority exists in the Church, despite the negative indications of the 2001 notification and the 2002 ITC document. Currently, the answer to the question of ordaining women seems to rest in the power of the episcopate, that is, in the power of the bishop to minister to his diocese. But perhaps the answer should rest in the recognition of episcopal autonomy rather than in lower-level discussion about the history of women deacons such as we find in these two recent documents.

Should a bishop choose to ordain a woman deacon (I have already established that he *can*), the question here examined—that of governance and ministry for women in the Catholic Church—would begin to be answered. Diaconal ministry includes ministry of the Word, the liturgy, and charity, so restoration of the ancient tradition of ordained women deacons in the Catholic Church would restore women to greater and more public means of engaging in formal, ordained ministry.

The neuralgic issues of the ministry of the Word and of the liturgy in general are somewhat obvious, as well as conjoined. While these ministries take on many forms, the most public and perhaps most contentious regarding women involve preaching during liturgies, particularly during the Liturgy of the Eucharist. Canon 767 restricts the homily to "*sacerdoti aut diacono*," that is, to bishops, priests, and deacons. An interpretation of canon 767.1 by the Pontifical Council on Interpretation of Legislative Texts (May 26, 1987) apparently overrides the dispensary power of the diocesan ordinary as specified in canon 87, and states that he cannot allow others to preach. While women do offer "reflections" at liturgies, ordained women deacons would preach— deliver a homily—formally and legally.[33]

And what would women deacons preach about? Charity. If women were restored to the ancient order of the diaconate, they would participate not only in the ministry of charity but also in its governance. That is, among the specific governing functions that could accrue to women deacons would be the legal and canonical financial oversight of the Church's treasure. That is part of the ancient ministry of the diaconate.

Often the ministry of charity by women indicates the hands-on ministry, the actual one-by-one charity of personalism Dorothy Day spoke of. But there are large sums of money involved in the Church's charity, and, technically speaking, only ordained persons can have authority over it. When Benedict spoke about "more space" for women in governance, this might indeed be one of the functions he was thinking about.

Another function for women that he may have been thinking about is women cardinals. The new Code of Canon Law requires priestly ordination for appointment, and subsequent ordination to episcopal rank if the cardinal-select is not already a bishop.[34] Cardinals can request they not be made bishops, and there is a long history of cardinal-deacons. Canon 231.2 of the 1917 Code of Canon Law provides for cardinals who are deacons. A return to the older tradition, perhaps through a simple derogation from the current law, would allow women deacons to be chosen as cardinals.[35]

WHICH WAY TO THE FUTURE?

In a public meeting with journalists and others the day or so after his 1988 talk at St. Peter's Lutheran Church, Cardinal Ratzinger, then prefect of the CDF, agreed that the God of philosophy is neither male nor female, and the God of theology is both. When pressed on the question of restoring the ancient tradition of ordained women deacons in the Catholic Church, he said it was "under study."[36]

That study had begun soon after the diaconate was formally restored as a permanent vocation in 1972 by Paul VI,[37] who asked the ITC to take up the question. (Ratzinger had been appointed to the ITC in 1969 and became its president in 1982.) The answer—reportedly in 1974—came in the affirmative but was never promulgated. Commission member Cipriano Vagaggini found that women deacons were ordained by the bishop in the presence of the presbyterate and within the sanctuary by the imposition of hands; Vagaggini published his positive historical analysis of women deacons in an Italian journal two years later.[38] Meanwhile, the ITC, under Ratzinger's leadership, labored for another twenty-eight years before publishing a document that was, at best, ambiguous.

When in 2002 the ITC finally presented a document on the diaconate—the document addressed earlier—it argued against the apparent original findings as published by Vagaggini. Even so, any determination about the restoration of the female diaconate belongs to the magisterium and, since the possibility of an affirmative determination has been demonstrated, one could realistically expect the magisterium to act affirmatively.

Logically, the decision of the magisterium—essentially of Benedict XVI—must be either affirmative or postponed. Neither of the two objections to women deacons was raised against the ordination of women as priests in the CDF's declaration *Inter Insigniores* (October 15, 1976).[39] The "*in persona Christi*" or the "iconic" argument (one must physically resemble the maleness of Christ in order to represent him) and the argument from "authority" (Jesus chose only male apostles) do not apply to the diaconate.

Even so, there has been a crossover from the argument against priestly ordination of women to the argument against diaconal ordination of women. But the iconic argument represents a naive physicalism that reduces Christ's humanity to maleness and ignores the overwhelming fact that God became human in Christ.[40] The iconic argument of *Inter Insigniores* remains troubling—and insulting. But Ratzinger's public response in 1988, that the God of philosophy is neither male nor female, and the God of theology is both, evicts the iconic argument from the mix. In fact, the iconic argument disappeared eighteen years after *Inter Insigniores* with John Paul II's *Ordinatio Sacerdotalis* (May 22, 1994), which retained only the argument from authority: "I declare that the Church has no authority whatsoever to confer priestly ordination on women and that this judgment is to be definitively held by all the Church's faithful."[41]

The present discussion, however, involves the diaconate. Does the Church have the power and the authority to ordain women deacons? Each of these two contemporary documents, *Inter Insigniores* and *Ordinatio Sacerdotalis*, about the ordination of women concerns priesthood. The former specifically leaves the discussion of the diaconate aside; the latter does not address the diaconate at all.

If the iconic argument has been dropped, then the argument from authority must be examined in full. Christ clearly had female helpers, but they are not named among the Twelve. However, it is quite clear that the community of believers called forth those now considered the first deacons, who then received the laying on of hands from the apostles (Acts 6:1–6). Therefore, the choice of deacons is up to the Church, to be confirmed by the successors to the apostles.

Romans 16:1–2 and 1 Timothy 3:11 both testify to the fact of women in the earliest stages of the diaconate.[42] In fact, Scripture names Phoebe, deacon and patron of the church at Cenchreae (Rom 16:1–2). Other female coworkers of Paul are named: Tryphaena, Tryphosa, and Persis (Rom 16:12); Euodia and Syntyche (Phil 4:2–3); Mary (Rom 16:6); and Junia, "a notable apostle" (Rom 16:7).

CONCLUSIONS

Independent of the discussion of women priests, it would seem that today the Church has both the "authority" —and the power—to ordain women deacons.

The terms Benedict XVI used on March 2, 2006, in Rome are quite clear. The pope, the principal teacher of the Church, has said that women may be able to enter into church governance and ministry. Strictly speaking, each requires ordination, but not necessarily priestly ordination.

In a German television interview broadcast August 13, 2006, Benedict repeated that women could not become priests because Christ chose only male apostles, but he seems to have indicated that canon law might change to allow women more power. The pope essentially reiterated his comments of March 2, 2006, adding: "But there's a juridical problem: according to Canon Law the power to take legally binding decisions is limited to Sacred Orders. So there are limitations from this point of view but I believe that women themselves, with their energy and strength, with their superiority, with what I'd call their 'spiritual power,' will know how to make their own space. And we will have to try and listen to God so as not to stand in their way."[43]

The Web site for Benedict's diocese of Rome states that there are 1,740 secular priests and 3,650 religious priests, for a total of 5,390 priests in the diocese. These numbers probably include the cardinal vicar general and the nine auxiliary bishops. The Web site also lists 88 deacons, but nowhere does it indicate how many secular or religious women serve the diocese.

But as recently as February 14, 2007, Benedict said, "Among the disciples many women were also chosen.... They played an active role within the context of Jesus' mission" and Paul's admonition against women "speaking in church" needed to be "relativized."[44]

It would seem that the sense of Benedict's words and his sense of history will eventually, if not immediately, enhance the Church's perspectives of both ministry and governance by the restoration of the female diaconate to the Catholic Church. At least that seems to be the direction of his comments.

NOTES

FOREWORD

1. Paul VI, *Hodie Concilium, AAS* 58 (1966): 57–64.

2. Paul VI, *Ad Pascendum* (August 15, 1972), citing Matt 20:28.

3. John Paul II, Allocution to the Permanent Deacons and Their Wives Given at Detroit, MI (September 19, 1987), *Origins* 17 (1987): 327–29.

4. *Acta Synodalia Sacrosancti Concilii Vaticani II* (Typis Polyglottis Vaticanis, 1970–), II/II, 317–19.

CHAPTER ONE

1. As quoted by John Paul II, apostolic letter *Mulieris Dignitatem* (August 15, 1988).

2. VOTF, the Boston-based group formed in response to scandals in the Archdiocese of Boston, aims to reform Church structure; LCWR is the principal association of leaders of women's religious communities in the United States; CTA defines itself as a national coalition of Catholics working for peace and justice in the Catholic Church and beyond.

3. In 1997, the number of parish lay ministers paid for at least twenty hours a week was 29,146, an increase of 35 percent since 1992. At that time, 82 percent of parish lay ministers were women. Philip J. Murnion and David DeLambo, *Parishes and Parish Ministers: A Study of Parish Lay Ministers* (New York: National

Pastoral Life Center, 1999). Newer statistics count 30,632 parish lay ministers paid for at least twenty hours per week, of whom 80 percent are women (of whom 16 percent are women religious). David DeLambo, *Lay Parish Ministers: A Study of Emerging Parish Leadership* (New York: National Pastoral Life Center, 2005), 44.

4. The Vatican Yearbook for 2002, *Annuario Pontificio per L'Anno* 2002 (Città del Vaticano: Tipografia Poliglotta Vaticana, 2004), noted 30,087 permanent deacons worldwide in both the Eastern and Latin Catholic Churches.

5. The exception would be Syro-Malabar Catholic, Syrian Catholic, and Coptic Catholic (except converts from Orthodoxy) priests, who must be celibate. Typically, Eastern Catholic priest-candidates for the United States and Australia must be celibate (*viz.* Pius XI, *Cum Data Fuerit* [March 1, 1929]), although in the twenty-first century there have been a few married men ordained priests by Byzantine, Ukrainian, Romanian, and Melkite bishops in the United States, and by Ukrainian bishops in Canada. See note 9, below.

6. Following the close of the Second Vatican Council, Pope Paul VI created the Synod of Bishops in 1965 to bring together the world's bishops for discussions of Church issues.

7. CORPUS, the national association for an inclusive priest-hood, is one of the older Catholic reform groups in the United States, founded in 1974; CITI Ministries was founded in 1992, and supports "Rent-a-Priest." CITI provides legal certification of priestly status, which allows priest-members to perform marriage ceremonies under civil authority, and sells a variety of items, including bumper stickers: "39 Popes Were Married," and "Married Priests Promote Family Values."

8. FutureChurch states it is a coalition of parish-based Catholics that works to preserve the Eucharist by advocating for opening ordination to all the baptized.

9. Married Eastern Catholic priests ordained outside North America are well accepted. See Roxanne King, "Married Byzantine priest to serve as administrator of downtown parish," *Denver Catholic Register*, June 4, 2003. In 1994, Ukrainian Bishop Basil Filevich of Saskatchewan, Canada, ordained married candidate

Ivan Nahachewsky to priesthood; in 1996, Melkite Catholic Bishop John Elya ordained married Protodeacon André St. Germain to priesthood in Methuen, Massachusetts. See "A Quiet Revolution" by William Bole at http://www.catholic.net/RCC/Periodicals/ Igpress/CWR/CWR0397/USA.html (accessed May 7, 2007). In 1999, the Vatican approved the Particular Law for the Byzantine-Ruthenian Church in the USA, which governs the Ruthenian Catholic Archdiocese of Pittsburgh and the Dioceses of Passaic, Parma, and Van Nuys. Canon 758.3 of the Particular Law provides for married U.S. priest candidates to be approved by Rome on a case-by-case basis.

10. There are as many as one hundred "Catholic" Churches, ranging from the American Catholic Church to the Universal Christian Catholic Church. Some claim valid succession through Union of Utrecht Old Catholic Churches, or through other lines. Some ordain women. Their clergy, when they ask to be admitted to the Catholic Church, are admitted as laypersons.

11. The growing Roman Catholic Womenpriest movement is reflective of this situation. Some persons ordained by this movement have joined communions that call themselves Catholic, but which are not in communion with Rome, and which have married male priests. The first U.S. ordination ceremonies for the Roman Catholic Womenpriest movement took place in Pittsburgh on July 31, 2006. A second round of North American ordinations (fourteen deacons, including two men, and nine priests) took place in 2007 in Quebec, Toronto, New York, Santa Barbara, Portland, and Minneapolis. http://www.romancatholicwomenpriests.org/events .htm (accessed July 28, 2007).

12. For example, James F. David, a former Roman Catholic priest, and his wife, Marie S. David, an ordained priest of Roman Catholic Womenpriest, have faculties from the Ecumenical Catholic Diocese of America (Peter Paul Brennan) and run a retreat center on Cape Cod. Peter Paul Brennan has twice been ordained priest (Old Roman Catholic Church in North America, and African Orthodox Church), has five times been ordained bishop (African Orthodox Church, Long Island; African Orthodox

Church, Brooklyn; Ecumenical Catholic Diocese of the Americas, Los Angeles; Iglesia Ortodoxa Católica Apostólica, Los Angeles); and is also Primate of the Order of Corporate Reunion (Queens, NY). Most recently, he was among the four men ordained as bishop by Archbishop Milingo in 2006.

13. This specific point, and the more general point of the general inability of some celibate priests to relate maturely to women, is discussed in a number of works. See, for example, Thomas P. Doyle, A. W. R. Sipe, and Patrick Wall, *Sex, Priests, and Secret Codes* (Los Angeles: Volt Press, 2006); Richard A. Schoenherr, *Goodbye Father: The Celibate Male Priesthood and the Future of the Catholic Church*, ed. David Yamane (New York: Oxford University Press, 2002).

14. Canons 492 and 537 govern the diocesan and parochial finance councils, respectively.

15. "With the exception of a comma, the final wording of para.1 in (what eventually became) canon 129 is exactly the wording that Cardinal Ratzinger had previously proposed." Elizabeth McDonough, "Jurisdiction Exercised by Non-Ordained Members in Religious Institutes," *Canon Law Society of America Proceedings* 58 (1996): 292–307, at 294 n4. McDonough refers to Cardinal Ratzinger's *animadversiones* and suggested text of December 22, 1980, as published in *Pontificium Consilium De Legum Textibus Interpretandis, Acta et Documenta Pontificae Commissionis Codici Iuris Canonici Recognoscendo, Congregatio Plenaria*, October 20–29, 1981 (Civitas Vaticana: Typis Polyglottia Vaticanis, 1991), 38–45.

16. In 1980, the Holy See created a pastoral provision for receiving former Episcopal priests in the United States, in some case with their congregations. Only in the seven Anglican Use congregations (five in Texas, one each in Massachusetts and South Carolina) does a former Episcopal priest act as "pastor." Since 1983, approximately 80 former Episcopal priests have been ordained as Catholic priests; most are married. See Paul VI, encyclical letter, *Sacerdotalis Coelebatis* (June 24, 1967), no. 42. In the United States and elsewhere, a few former Protestant ministers are also married Roman Catholic priests, but accurate statistics are

difficult to come by. There are 600 former Anglican Catholic priests in the United Kingdom (150 married) and a few in Spain. See Dwight Longenecker, "The Anglican Right," *Crisis Magazine*, June 13, 2007. http://www.crisismagazine.com/june2007/longenecker.htm (accessed July 28, 2007).

17. From *The Official Catholic Directory 2006* (New Providence, NJ: P. J. Kenedy & Sons, 2006) and *Statistical Yearbook of the Church 2004* (Civitas Vaticana: Typis Polyglottis Vaticanis, 2004); population estimated as of June 30, 2002.

18. At the 2005 Synod of Bishops, the organization Future-Church presented a petition with 35,000 signatures asking for discussion of married priests and women deacons. Of the 314 members and observers of the Synod, fourteen were women auditors who had no voice in the Synod.

19. *Definitive* applied to divinely revealed doctrine is distinct from *definitive* applied to official Church teaching that must be held, including infallible statements. However, as James Provost points out, "The canons do try to provide a protection against a creeping infallibilism: 'No doctrine is understood to be infallibly defined unless it is clearly established as such' (Canon 749 §3). They also require a 'definitive act' for the pope to declare something infallibly. Definitive teaching, in the code, is another way of saying that a teaching has been declared infallibly even in the *tenenda* category." James H. Provost, "Safeguarding the Faith," *America*, August 1, 1998, 12.

20. Canon 749.3: "No doctrine is understood as defined infallibly unless this is manifestly evident." See Catholic Theological Society of America, "Tradition and the Ordination of Women," *Origins* 27:5 (June 19, 1997): 75–79.

21. See Phyllis Zagano, "The Revisionist History of Benedict XVI," *Harvard Divinity Bulletin* 34, no. 2 (Spring 2006): 72–77, at 74.

22. International Theological Commission, *From Diakonia of Christ to the Diakonia of the Apostles* (Chicago: Hillenbrand Books, 2006).

23. "In the history of the Church, even from earliest times, there were side-by-side with men a number of women, for whom

the response of the Bride to the Bridegroom's redemptive love acquired full expressive force. First we see those women who had personally encountered Christ and followed him. After his departure, together with the Apostles, they 'devoted themselves to prayer' in the Upper Room in Jerusalem until the day of Pentecost. On that day the Holy Spirit spoke through 'the sons and daughters' of the People of God, thus fulfilling the words of the prophet Joel (cf. *Acts* 2:17). These women, and others afterwards, played an active and important role in the life of the early Church, in building up from its foundations the first Christian community—and subsequent communities—through their own charisms and their varied service. The apostolic writings note their names, such as Phoebe, 'a deaconess of the Church at Cenchreae' (cf. *Rom* 16:1), Prisca with her husband Aquila (cf. *2 Tim* 4:19), Euodia and Syntyche (cf. *Phil* 4:2), Mary, Tryphaena, Persis, and Tryphosa (cf. *Rom* 16:6, 12). Saint Paul speaks of their 'hard work' for Christ, and this hard work indicates the various fields of the Church's apostolic service, beginning with the 'domestic Church.' For in the latter, 'sincere faith' passes from the mother to her children and grandchildren, as was the case in the house of Timothy (cf. *2 Tim* 1:5)." John Paul II, apostolic letter *Mulieris Dignitatem* (August 15, 1988), 27. Other translators of Romans 16:1 correctly call Phoebe a deacon, not a deaconess, of the Church at Cenchreae.

24. Francis Schüssler Fiorenza, "From Theologian to Pope: A personal view back, past the public portrayals," *Harvard Divinity Bulletin* 33, no. 2 (Autumn 2005).

25. See, for example, Roger Gryson, *The Ministry of Women in the Early Church* (Collegeville, MN: Liturgical Press, 1976), the translation of *Le ministère des femmes dans L'Église ancienne. Recherches et synthèses, Section d'historire* 4 (Gembloux: J. Duculot, 1972); Aimé Georges Martimort, *Deaconesses: An Historical Study* (San Francisco: Ignatius, 1986), the translation of *Les Diaconesses: Essai Historique* (Rome: Edizioni Liturgiche, 1982); Phyllis Zagano, *Holy Saturday: An Argument for the Restoration of the Female Diaconate in the Catholic Church* (New York: Crossroad, 2000); Ute Eisen, *Women Officeholders in Early Christianity: Epigraphical and Literary Studies*

(Collegeville, MN: Liturgical Press, 2000), the translation of *Amsträgerinnen im frühen Christentum. Epigraphische und literarische Studien* (Göttingen: Vandenhoeck & Ruprecht, 1996); and Kevin Madigan and Carolyn Osiek, *Ordained Women in the Catholic Church: A Documentary History* (Baltimore: Johns Hopkins University, 2005).

26. The Holy Synod of the Orthodox Church of Greece voted in October 2004 to restore the monastic female diaconate, although there was discussion about a ministerial female diaconate. "Church steps back to the future," *Kathimerini English Daily*, October 9, 2004; ANA English-language section of October 9; http://www.hri.org/news/greek/ana/2004/04-10-09.ana.html#14. See also Phyllis Zagano, "Grant Her Your Spirit: The Restoration of the Female Diaconate in the Orthodox Church of Greece," *America*, February 7, 2005, 18–21; translated as "Chiesa Ortodossa Geca: Il ripristino del diaconato femminile," *Adista* (26 febbraio 2005).

27. This admittedly weak argument is proposed for women priests by John Wijngaards, *Women Deacons in the Early Church: Historical Texts and Early Debates* (Crossroad, 2006). Some Union of Utrecht Old Catholic Churches ordain both women deacons and women priests. The Armenian Apostolic Church and the Orthodox Church of Greece allow only the ordination of women deacons.

28. "If, because of a lack of priests, the diocesan bishop has decided that participation in the exercise of the pastoral care of a parish is to be entrusted to a deacon, to another person who is not a priest, or to a community of persons, he is to appoint some priest who, provided with the powers and faculties of a pastor, is to direct the pastoral care" (canon 517.2).

29. A Mexican Franciscan bishop now working in Peru evidenced the same attitude privately. He said he had no problem in ordaining married men to the priesthood or women to the diaconate.

30. Installation post-1983 applies only to the ministries of acolyte and lector. The ordinary means by which a person enters the clerical state, since 1983, is through ordination to the diaconate.

31. "An important issue for women is how to have a voice in the governance of the Church to which they belong and which

they serve with love and generosity. This can be achieved in at least two ways that are consistent with church teaching: through consultation and through cooperation in the exercise of authority." National Conference of Catholic Bishops, "Strengthening the Bonds of Peace: A Pastoral Reflection on Women in the Church and in Society" (Washington, DC: United States Catholic Conference, 1995). Susan Muto of Duquesne University was principal writer of the document. The ad hoc committee for the pastoral letter was headed by Bishop Joseph L. Imesch of Joliet, Illinois; the committee head for the statement was Bishop John Snyder, then bishop of St. Augustine. A strong member of the committee was Cardinal William J. Levada, now head of the Congregation for the Doctrine of the Faith.

32. Canon 129: "1. Those who have received sacred orders are qualified, according to the norm of the prescripts of the law, for the power of governance, which exists in the Church by divine institution and is also called the power of jurisdiction. 2. Lay members of the Christian faithful can cooperate in the exercise of this same power according to the norm of law."

33. Derogations would also be necessary to install women as acolytes and as lectors. Canon Law Society of America, *The Canonical Implications of Ordaining Women to the Permanent Diaconate* (Washington, DC, 1995).

34. *Notificazione delle Congregazioni per la Dottrina della Fede, per il Culto Divino e la Disciplina dei Sacramenti, per il Clero*: 1. Da taluni Paesi sono pervenute ai nostri Dicasteri alcune segnalazioni di programmazione e di svolgimento di corsi, direttamente o indirettamente finalizzati all'ordinazione diaconale delle donne. Si vengono così a determinare aspettative carenti di salda fondatezza dottrinale e che possono generare, pertanto, disorientamento pastorale. 2. Poiché l'ordinamento ecclesiale non prevede la possibilità di una tale ordinazione, non è lecito porre in atto iniziative che, in qualche modo, mirino a preparare candidate all'Ordine diaconale. 3. L'autentica promozione della donna nella Chiesa, in conformità al costante Magistero ecclesiastico, con speciale riferimento a quello di Sua Santità Giovanni Paolo II, apre altre ampie

prospettive di servizio e di collaborazione. 4. Le Congregazioni sottoscritte—nell'ambito delle proprie competenze—si rivolgono, pertanto, ai singoli Ordinari affinché vogliano spiegare ai propri fedeli ed applicare diligentemente la suindicata direttiva. Questa Notificazione è stata approvata dal Santo Padre, il 14 settembre 2001. Dal Vaticano, 17 settembre 2001. (Original text.) Each signer voted in the 2005 papal conclave: Cardinals Joseph Ratzinger (head of the Congregation for the Doctrine of the Faith, now Benedict XVI), Jorge Arturo Medina Estévez (head of Divine Worship and the Discipline of the Sacraments, now retired), and Darío Castrillón Hoyos (head of Clergy, and president of the Pontifical Commission Ecclesia Dei), and one was elected pope.

35. Translated by the author from the French: "Pour ce qui est de l'ordination des femmes au diaconat, il convient de noter que deux indications importantes émergent de ce qui a été exposé jusqu'ici: 1) les deaconesses dont il est fait mention dans la Tradition de l'Église ancienne—selon ce que suggèrent le rite d'institution et les functions exercées—ne sont pas purement et simplement assimilables aux diacres; 2) l'unité du sacrament de l'ordre, dans la claire distinction entre les ministères de l'évêque et des presbyters d'une part et le ministère diaconal d'autre part, est fortement souligné par la Tradition ecclésiale, surtout dans la doctrine du Concile Vatican II et l'enseignement postconciliare du Magistère. À la lumière de ces éléments mis en évidence par la présente recherche historico-théologique, il reviendra au ministère de discernement que le Seigneur a établi dans son Église de se prononcer avec autorité sur la question." "Le Diaconat," *La documentation catholique* (19 janvier 2003), 23:107. The Commission maintains the singular "order" found in *Catéchisme de l'Église catholique*. English language canon law (cc. 1008–54) uses "orders" and the *Catechism of the Catholic Church* (ch. 3, art. 6) uses "holy orders." The original language of the ITC document is French. It was first published as "Le Diaconat: Évolution et perspectives," *La documentation catholique* 23 (19 janvier 2003): 58–107; and in Italian, "Il Diaconato: Evoluzione e Prospettive," *La Civiltà Cattolica* 1 (2003): 253–336.

36. See Phyllis Zagano, "Catholic Women Deacons: Present Tense," *Worship* 77:5 (September 2003): 386–408.

37. See Phyllis Zagano, "Grant Her Your Spirit: The Restoration of the Female Diaconate in the Orthodox Church of Greece," *America*, February 7, 2005, 18–21. Translated as "Chiesa Ortodossa Geca: Il ripristino del diaconato femminile," *Adista* (26 febbraio 2005).

38. Founded in 1960, the Standing Conference of the Canonical Orthodox Bishops in the Americas (SCOBA) brings together nine canonical hierarchs of Orthodox jurisdictions in the Americas: the Albanian Orthodox Diocese of America, Antiochian Orthodox Christian Archdiocese of North America, Bulgarian Eastern Orthodox Church, Carpatho-Russian Orthodox Diocese of the USA, Greek Orthodox Archdiocese of America, Orthodox Church in America, Romanian Orthodox Archdiocese in the Americas, Serbian Orthodox Church in North and South America, and Ukrainian Orthodox Church of the USA. Its offices are in New York.

39. Among the leaders of this group is Kyriaki K. FitzGerald, whose *Women Deacons in the Orthodox Church: Called to Holiness and Ministry* (Brookline, MA: Holy Cross Orthodox Press, 1998) is the definitive work on the topic in English.

40. Some of these issues are considered in Phyllis Zagano, "Women Religious, Women Deacons?" *Review for Religious* (May–June 2001): 230–44.

41. Rarely, usually in mission territories, laypersons are granted authority to baptize by rescript.

CHAPTER TWO

1. As in formal ecumenical dialogue, churches here are referred to as they term themselves. The Church headquartered at the Vatican refers to itself as the Catholic Church, not the Roman Catholic Church.

2. On May 27, 1996, German Old Catholic Bishop Joachim Vobbe ordained Old Catholic Deacons Regina Pickel-Bossau and

Angela Berlis to priesthood. Vobbe issued *"Geh zu meinen Brüdern"* (Bonn, 1996), which argues the case for the ordination of women. See "Pastoral Letter on Women's Ordination," http://www.ecumenical-catholic-communion.org/eccpdf/women.pdf (accessed April 22, 2010).

3. The Old Catholic Church of Switzerland first ordained women deacons about 1991 and priests in 2002.

4. Pius XII, apostolic constitution *Sacramentum Ordinis* (1947), http://www.papalencyclicals.net/Pius12/P12SACRAO.HTM (accessed April 16, 2010). See also *The Christian Faith in the Doctrinal Documents of the Catholic Church*, ed. J. Neuner and J. Dupuis (Bangalore: Theological Publications in India, 1991), 554.

5. See, for example, Roger Gryson, *The Ministry of Women in the Early Church*, trans. Jean Laporte and Mary Luise Hall (Collegeville, MN: Liturgical Press, 1976 [orig.: *Le ministère des femmes dans L'Église ancienne. Recherches et synthèses, Section d'histoire* 4 (Gembloux, BE: J. Duculot, 1972)]); Aimé George Martimort, *Deaconesses: An Historical Study*, trans. K. D. Whitehead (San Francisco: Ignatius Press, 1986 [orig.: *Les Diaconesses: Essai Historique* (Rome: Edizioni Liturgiche, 1982)]); Ute Eisen, *Women Officeholders in Early Christianity: Epigraphical and Literary Studies*, trans. Linda M. Maloney (Collegeville, MN: Liturgical Press, 2000 [orig.: *Amtsträgerinnen im frühen Christentum. Epigraphische und literarische Studien* (Göttingen: Vandenhoeck & Ruprecht, 1996)]); and Kevin Madigan and Carolyn Osiek, eds. and trans., *Ordained Women in the Catholic Church: A Documentary History* (Baltimore: Johns Hopkins University Press, 2005).

6. Paul VI, *Ad Pascendum* (August 15, 1972). *Acta Apostolicae Sedis* 64 (1972): 529–34.

7. The Catholic Church produces several levels of documents with varying levels of authority. The highest level documents are those of ecumenical councils. Documents issued by curial offices are regulatory but not necessarily legislative, and in no way approach the level of conciliar or even papal documents. A declaration is a curial pronouncement "which is an interpretation of existing law or facts, or a reply to a contested point of law or doc-

trine." Francis G. Morrissey, *Papal and Curial Pronouncements: Their Canonical Significance in Light of the Code of Canon Law*, 2nd ed. (Ottawa: Faculty of Canon Law, Saint Paul University, 1995), 29.

8. Apostolic epistles, or letters, "contain social and pastoral teachings, but are not legislative texts." Morrissey, *Papal and Curial Pronouncements*, 13.

9. Canon 749.3: "No doctrine is understood as defined infallibly unless this is manifestly evident." Available at http://www.vatican.va/archive/ENG1104/__P2H.HTM.

10. The International Theological Commission document has been published in French ("*Le Diaconat: Évolution et perspectives*," *La documentation catholique* 23 [19 janvier 2003]: 58–107) and Italian ("*Il Diaconato: Evoluzione e Prospettive*," *La Civiltà Cattolica*, vol. I [2003], 253–336). An unofficial English translation was published in London: "From the Diakonoia of Christ to the Diakonoia of the Apostles," by the Catholic Truth Society in 2003. The official French-language document is on the Vatican Web site.

11. Nicaea (325) and Chalcedon (451). Chalcedon lowered the minimum age for the ordination of women deacons from sixty to forty. See Madigan and Osiek, *Ordained Women in the Early Church: A Documentary History*, 121–23.

12. From a letter of Pope Benedict VII to Benedict, bishop of Porto: "In the same way, we concede and confirm to you and your successors in perpetuity every episcopal ordination (*ordinationem episcopalem*), not only of presbyters but also of deacons or deaconesses (*diaconissis*) or subdeacons." Ibid., 147.

13. A joint notification issued by the Catholic Congregations for the Doctrine of the Faith, for Worship and Sacraments, and for the Clergy essentially reminded diocesan ordinaries that women were not to be trained as deacons, since they did not envision ordaining them. Cardinal Joseph Ratzinger was among the signers. A notification is not a legislative document. See Morrissey, *Papal and Curial Pronouncements*, 36. For the full original text, see note 34 for chapter 1 herein.

14. From the official church calendar published by the Armenian Patriarchate of Turkey: "Mother Hrip'sime Protodeacon

Sasunian, born in Soghukoluk, Antioch, in 1928; became a nun in 1953; Protodeacon in 1984; Mother Superior in 1998. Member of the Kalfayian Order." *Oratsuyts'* (Istanbul: Armenian Patriarchate, 2001), 254, trans. Fr. Krikor Maksoudian.

15. See Abel Oghlukian, *The Deaconess in the Armenian Church*, trans. S. Peter Cowe (New Rochelle, NY: St. Nersess, 1993). A history of women deacons in the Armenian Church is presented in M. Kristin Arat, "*Die diakonissen der armenischen Kirche in kanonischer Sicht,*" *Handes Amsorya* (1987), 153–89.

16. The ecumenical councils generally agreed to by all Christendom (except for the Oriental Orthodox, which recognizes only the first three, and the Assyrian Church of the East, which recognizes only the first two) are: Nicaea (325 AD), Constantinople (381), Ephesus (430), Chalcedon (451), Constantinople (553), Constantinople (680), and Nicaea (787). The Armenians did not attend councils after 430.

17. See Timothy Ware, *The Orthodox Church*, 2nd ed. (New York and London: Penguin Books, 1997).

18. The Joint International Commission for Theological Dialogue between the Catholic Church and the Orthodox Church approved the common statement in its fifth plenary session at the monastery of New Valamo, Finland, June 19–27, 1988. The quotation is from no. 1; see http://www.vatican.va/roman_curia/pontifical _councils/chrstuni/ch_orthodox_docs/rc_pc_chrstuni_doc_1988 0626_finland_en.html.

19. Ibid., no. 43.

20. Congregation for the Doctrine of the Faith, *Inter Insigniores* (October 15, 1976), no. 5.

21. The 1886 *Caeremoniale Episcoporum*, revised after the Second Vatican Council, retains the older tradition. "The vestments worn by the bishop at a liturgical celebration are the same as those worn by presbyters; but in accordance with traditional usage, it is fitting that at a solemn celebration he wear under the chasuble a dalmatic (which may always be white). This applies particularly to the celebration of ordinations, the blessing of an abbot or abbess, and the dedication of a church and an altar."

Ceremonial of Bishops (Collegeville, MN: Liturgical Press, 1989), part I, chap. 4, no. 56, p. 33.

22. St. Nectarios the Wonderworker was metropolitan of Pentapolis briefly, but was removed from office in 1890. He became an educator in Greece and in 1904 founded a female monastery, the Holy Trinity Convent in Aegina, to which he retired in 1908. His body was found incorrupt after death. The Orthodox Church declared him a saint in 1961.

23. "Church steps back to the future," *Kathimerini English Daily*, October 9, 2004; ANA English-language section of October 9. See http://www.hri.org/news/greek/ana/2004/04-10-09.ana.html#14.

24. Phyllis Zagano, "Grant Her Your Spirit: The Restoration of the Female Diaconate in the Orthodox Church of Greece," *America* (February 7, 2005), 18–21; translated as *"Chiesa Ortodossa Greca: Il ripristino del diaconato femminile," Adista* (26 febbraio 2005).

25. United States Catholic Conference, Bishops' Committee on Ecumenical and Interreligious Affairs, "Pastoral Guidelines Concerning Admission of Polish National Catholics to Sacraments in the Roman Catholic Church (canon 844)."

26. Iglesia Filipina Independiente broke from Rome in 1902. The Bonn Agreement of July 2, 1931, established intercommunion (now referred to as "full communion") between the Old Catholic Churches of the Union of Utrecht and the Church of England.

27. Among the others that use the term *Old Catholic* in the United States are the Old Catholic Church of America, the Old Catholic Church in North America, the Catholic Apostolic National Church, and the Independent Old Catholic Church of America. The Catholic Church technically recognizes the validity of orders in the autocephalous church movement (the Catholic Apostolic Church), which has ordained women since the 1960s, but since it receives persons ordained by the movement as laypersons, it has made no statement regarding the validity of women's ordination within the movement.

28. Martina Schneibergova, Jana Sustova, et al., *"Die altkatholische Kirche hat ihre erste Diakonin,"* Radio Praha (October

30, 2003): "Die altkatholische Kirche in Tschechien hat unter ihren Geistlichen die erste Frau. Über die Weihe der ersten Diakonin durch den altkatholischen Bischof Dusan Hejbal berichtet Martina Schneibergova." Text of report is at http://radio.cz/de/artikel/46864.

29. Ludmila Javorová (b. 1932) was secretly ordained a Roman Catholic priest in 1970 by Bishop Felix Maria Davidek (1921–88) in the Czechoslovakian underground Koinótés fellowship. Several other men and women were ordained as deacons and priests. The Catholic Church considers Bishop Davidek an affiliated bishop of the Diocese of Brno, Moravia, Czech Republic. The Catholic Congregation for the Doctrine of the Faith declared the secret ordinations illicit in February 2000, and regularized fifty celibate and twenty-two married men by reordaining them "sub-conditione," but never directly made any statement about the ordained women. See Congregation for the Doctrine of the Faith, Declaration, "On Bishops and Priests Ordained Secretly in the Czech Republic" (February 11, 2000). Javorová was not invited to be reordained, although apparently her bishop asked her not to exercise priestly ministry, and she has complied. As many as five other women were ordained, some solely to the diaconate. See Miriam Therese Winter, *Out of the Depths: The Story of Ludmila Javorova, Ordained Roman Catholic Priest* (New York: Crossroad, 2001); Petr Fiala and Jiří Hanuš, *Skrytá církev, Felix M. Davídek a společenství Koinótés* (Brno, Czech Republic: CDK, 1999).

30. See note 10, above.

31. See Gryson, *The Ministry of Women in the Early Church*, 62, citing F. X. Funk, *Didascalia et constitutions Apostolorum*, 2 vols. (Paderborn: 1905; reprint Turin: 1964), 524, 13–24. The earliest known ordination ritual for a woman deacon is present in the *Apostolic Constitutions*. See Paul F. Bradshaw, *Ordination Rites of the Ancient Churches of East and West* (New York: Pueblo Publishing Company, 1990), 116. See also Ecumenical Patriarchate, *The Place of Women in the Orthodox Church and the Question of the Ordination of Women*, Report of the Interorthodox Symposium, Rhodos (Rhodes), Greece (October 10–November 7, 1988), ed. Gennadios Limouris

(Katerini, Greece: Tertios Publications, 1992), 31–32. The liturgical text as reconstructed by Jacob Goar, in *Euchologion sive Rituale Graecorum* (Paris) 1647, 262–64, reflects the liturgy likely to be used. Goar reconstructed the ancient formulae of Greek liturgy using seven manuscripts, most probably Barberini, Grottaferrata, St. Mark (Florence), Tillianus, Allatianus, Coresianus, and the Royal Library (France), as follows: "Holy and Omnipotent Lord, through the birth of your Only Son our God from a Virgin according to the flesh, you have sanctified woman. You grant not only to men, but also to women the grace and coming of the Holy Spirit. Please also now, Lord, look on this your maid servant and dedicate her to the task of your diaconate, and pour out into her the abundant giving of your Holy Spirit. Preserve her while she performs her ministry according to what is pleasing to you, in the orthodox faith and irreproachable conduct. For to you is due all glory, honor and worship, Father, Son and Holy Spirit, now and always and in all ages. Amen." Note that the woman deacon is ordained to ministry. (Trans. by John Wijngaards, http://www.womenpriests.org/traditio/deac_gr4.htm.)

32. "When the question of the ordination of women arose in the Anglican Communion, Pope Paul VI, out of fidelity to his office of safeguarding the Apostolic Tradition, and also with a view to removing a new obstacle placed in the way of Christian unity, reminded Anglicans of the position of the Catholic Church: 'She holds that it is not admissible to ordain women to the priesthood, for very fundamental reasons. These reasons include: the example recorded in the Sacred Scriptures of Christ choosing his Apostles only from among men; the constant practice of the Church, which has imitated Christ in choosing only men; and her living teaching authority which has consistently held that the exclusion of women from the priesthood is in accordance with God's plan for his Church.'" John Paul II, apostolic letter *Ordinatio Sacerdotalis*, May 22, 1994, quoting Paul VI, Response to the Letter of His Grace the Most Reverend Dr. F. D. Coggan, Archbishop of Canterbury, concerning the Ordination of Women to the Priesthood (November 30, 1975); *Acta Apostolicae Sedis*, vol. 68 (1976), 599.

33. Speaking at an ecumenical congress at Ushaw College, Durham, England, Cardinal Walter Kasper, president of the Pontifical Council for the Promotion of Christian Unity, pointed out that differences within Christianity over moral issues—he specifically noted homosexuality, abortion, and euthanasia—"are not on the top of the hierarchy of truths but they are very emotional and, therefore, very divisive." *Catholic News Service*, January 13, 2006.

34. Tracy Early, "Ecumenism undergoing 'radical change' in 21st century, cardinal says," *Catholic News Service*, March 17, 2005.

35. Ibid.

36. See Code of Canon Law: c. 767.1: "Among the forms of preaching, the homily…is part of the liturgy itself and is reserved to a priest or deacon…." Canon 274.1: "Only clerics can obtain offices for whose exercise the power of orders or the power of ecclesiastical governance is required."

37. "…the deaconesses mentioned in the ancient tradition of the Church—as suggested by their rite of institution and the functions they exercised—are not purely and simply the same as deacons…"; in the original document: "…les deaconesses dont il est fait mention dans la Tradition de l'Église ancienne—selon ce que suggèrent le rite d'institution et les functions exercées—ne sont pas purement et simplement assimilables aux diacres…" *("Le Diaconat," La documentation catholique*, 107). My translation.

CHAPTER THREE

1. This article is based on papers delivered during the Great Women of the Spirit Week at Regis University, Denver, Colorado, March 23, 2006, and the annual meeting of Voice of the Faithful of Long Island, April 22, 2006.

2. "'Sintesi degli interventi dei sacerdoti romani ricevuti in udienza dal Papa,' Vatican, Friday, March 3, 2006 (ZENIT.org). Pubblichiamo di seguito la sintesi degli interventi dei sacerdoti che

hanno preso la parola nel corso dell'udienza di Benedetto XVI al Clero della Diocesi di Roma, tenutasi il 2 marzo....

"Don Marco Valentini, vicario parrocchiale di san Girolamo a Corviale (Settore Ovest, XXXI Prefettura), ha pronunciato un intervento ispirato alla conoscenza avuta di una madre di famiglia e di alcune suore impegnate nel recupero di sacerdoti in crisi. 'Tale esperienza mi ha fatto pensare—ha detto—: perché non affiancare anche la donna al governo della Chiesa? Del resto il suo punto di vista nelle decisioni da prendere è diverso da quello maschile. La donna spesso lavora a livello carismatico con la preghiera o a livello pratico, come ha fatto santa Caterina da Siena che ha riportato il Papa a Roma. Perciò, occorrerebbe rilanciarne il ruolo anche a livello istituzionale e vedere il punto di vista della donna che è diverso da quello maschile, per aiutare non solo i sacerdoti in difficoltà, ma tutti i presbiteri quando devono prendere decisioni impegnative'" (http://www.zenit.org/italian/visualizza.php?sid=7281 [accessed February 27, 2007]).

3. Here Benedict refers to the optional list of women martyrs in the Commemoration of the Dead, which comes after the consecration: "For ourselves, too, we ask some share in the fellowship of your apostles and martyrs, with John the Baptist, Stephen, Matthias, Barnabas, (Ignatius, Alexander, Marcellinus, Peter, Felicity, Perpetua, Agatha, Lucy, Agnes, Cecilia, Anastasia) and all the saints." The priest then continues: "Though we are sinners, we trust in your mercy and love. Do not consider what we truly deserve, but grant us your forgiveness."

4. In the text supplied by ZENIT and the Vatican (see nn. 5 and 6 below), Benedict says, "cominciando dalle suore, dalle sorelle dei grandi Padri della Chiesa." In using the word *suore* (religious sisters), Benedict seems to have misspoken and then immediately corrected himself with "sorelle" (blood sisters). Thus, my translation omits as unintended the reference to religious sisters antecedent to the reference to sisters of Church Fathers.

5. My translation: "Discorso improvvisato da Benedetto XVI al Clero romano: I temi dell'incontro: vita, famiglia e formazione dei sacerdoti," March 2, 2006, reported by ZENIT on March 3, 2006: http://www.zenit.org/italian/visualizza.php? sid=7283 (accessed February 4, 2007):

Il 2 marzo 2006, nell'Aula della Benedizione del Palazzo Apostolico Vaticano, Benedetto XVI ha incontrato il Clero della Diocesi di Roma per il tradizionale appuntamento di inizio Quaresima. Di seguito riportiamo il testo improvvisato—in due tempi—dal Papa in risposta alle considerazioni dei sacerdoti romani intervenuti.

…Rispondo ora al vice Parroco di san Girolamo— vedo che è anche molto giovane—che ci parla di quanto fanno le donne nella Chiesa, anche proprio per i sacerdoti. Posso solo sottolineare che mi fa sempre grande impressione, nel primo Canone, quello Romano, la speciale preghiera per i sacerdoti: "Nobis quoque peccatoribus." Ecco, in questa umiltà realistica dei sacerdoti noi, proprio come peccatori, preghiamo il Signore perché ci aiuti ad essere suoi servi. In questa preghiera per il sacerdote, proprio solo in questa, appaiono sette donne che circondano il sacerdote. Esse si mostrano proprio come le donne credenti che ci aiutano nel nostro cammino. Ognuno ha certamente questa esperienza. E così la Chiesa ha un grande debito di ringraziamento per le donne. E giustamente Lei ha sottolineato che, a livello carismatico, le donne fanno tanto, oserei dire, per il governo della Chiesa, cominciando dalle suore, dalle sorelle dei grandi Padri della Chiesa, come sant'Ambrogio, fino alle grandi donne del medioevo—santa Ildegarda, santa Caterina da Siena, poi santa Teresa d'Avila—e fino a Madre Teresa. Direi che questo settore carismatico certamente si distingue dal settore ministeriale nel senso stretto della parola, ma è una vera e profonda partecipazione al governo della Chiesa. Come si potrebbe immaginare il governo della Chiesa senza questo contributo, che talvolta diventa molto visibile, come quando santa Ildegarda critica i Vescovi, o come quando santa Brigida e santa Caterina da Siena ammoniscono e ottengono il ritorno dei Papi a Roma? Sempre è un fattore determinante, senza il quale la Chiesa non può vivere. Tuttavia, giustamente Lei dice: vogliamo vedere anche più visibilmente in modo ministeriale le donne nel governo della Chiesa. Diciamo che la questione è questa. Il ministero sacerdotale dal Signore è, come sappiamo, riservato agli uomini, in quanto il ministero sacerdotale è governo nel senso profondo che, in definitiva, è il Sacramento che governa la Chiesa. Questo è il punto decisivo. Non è l'uomo che fa qualcosa, ma il sacerdote fedele alla sua missione governa, nel senso che è il Sacramento, cioè mediante il Sacramento è Cristo stesso che governa, sia tramite l'Eucaristia che negli altri Sacramenti, e così sempre Cristo presiede. Tuttavia, è giusto chiedersi se anche nel servizio ministeriale—nonostante il fatto che qui Sacramento e carisma siano il binario unico nel quale si realizza la Chiesa—non si possa offrire più spazio, più posizioni di responsabilità alle donne.

6. http://212.77.1.245/news_services/bulletin/news/18065.php?index=18065&po_date=03.03.2006&lang=it (accessed February 4, 2007).

7. National Conference of Catholic Bishops, "Strengthening the Bonds of Peace: A Pastoral Reflection on Women in the Church and in Society" (Washington, DC: United States Catholic Conference, 1995). Susan Muto of Duquesne University was the principal writer of the document. The ad hoc Committee on Women in Society and in the Church of the then–National Conference of Catholic Bishops was headed by Bishop Joseph L. Imesch of Joliet, Illinois; the head of the committee was Bishop John Snyder of St. Augustine, Florida. Bishop William J. Levada,

now cardinal prefect of the CDF, served on the committee. On May 13, 2005, he was appointed to the CDF by Pope Benedict XVI, with whom he worked closely at the CDF in the early 1980s.

8. Benedict XVI, *"Discorso improvvisato."*

9. This restriction applies to church governance in the ordinary sense. Abbesses and religious superiors hold the power of governance or the power of jurisdiction within their orders or institutes. Monastic prioresses and territorial abbesses retain additional authority within their properties. There and only there is exception made for a layperson (i.e., a religious brother) to have some jurisdiction over a cleric (i.e., an ordained member of a religious institute) and only in nonclerical matters.

10. "With the exception of a comma, the final wording of para. 1 in (what eventually became) canon 129 is exactly the wording that Cardinal Ratzinger had previously proposed." Elizabeth McDonough, "Jurisdiction Exercised by Non-Ordained Members in Religious Institutes," *Canon Law Society of America Proceedings of the Annual Convention* 58 (1996): 292–307, at 294 n. 4. McDonough refers to Cardinal Ratzinger's *animadversiones* and suggested text of December 22, 1980, in *Congregatio Plenaria.*

11. The ecumenical councils generally agreed to by all Christendom (except for the Oriental Orthodox, who recognize only the first three, and the Assyrian Church of the East, which recognizes only the first two) are: Nicaea (325), Constantinople (381), Ephesus (430), Chalcedon (451), Constantinople (553), Constantinople (680), and Nicaea (787).

12. "But if any have formerly been numbered among the clergy, if in fact they seem blameless and without reproach, when they have been rebaptized, let them be ordained by the bishop of the Catholic Church....And likewise, concerning the deaconesses... the same pattern should be observed" (Council of Nicaea, canon 19, quoted in Kevin Madigan and Carolyn Osiek, *Ordained Women in the Catholic Church: A Documentary History* (Baltimore: Johns Hopkins University, 2005), 117–18.

13. Ibid., 121–22.

14. See, e.g., Roger Gryson, *The Ministry of Women in the*

Early Church, trans. Jean Laporte and Mary Louise Hall (Collegeville, MN: Liturgical Press, 1976); Aimé George Martimort, *Deaconesses: An Historical Study*, trans. K. D. Whitehead (San Francisco: Ignatius Press, 1986); Ute Eisen, *Women Officeholders in Early Christianity: Epigraphical and Literary Studies*, trans. Linda M. Maloney (Collegeville, MN: Liturgical Press, 2000); and Madigan and Osiek, *Ordained Women*.

15. Madigan and Osiek, *Ordained Women*, 147. Their footnote states that the letter comes from Migne, PL 139.1921 and is also reproduced in *Monumenta de viduis diaconissis virginibusque tractantia*, ed. Josephine Mayer, Florilegium patristicum 42 (Bonn: Peter Hanstein, 1938), 52, and that Pope Leo IX later reconfirmed this concession (PL 143–602).

16. See John Paul II, apostolic letter for the Fourth Centenary of the Union of Brest, November 12, 1995: "Real, if imperfect communion, already present between Catholics and Orthodox in their ecclesial life, reaches perfection in all that we 'consider the highest point of the life of grace, *martyria* unto death, the truest communion possible with Christ who shed his Blood, and by that sacrifice brings near those who once were far off (cf. *Eph* 2:13),'" citing John Paul II, *Ut Unum Sint* no. 84, http://www.vatican.va/holy_father/john_paul_ii/apost_letters/documents/hf_jp-ii_apl_19951112_iv-cent-union-brest_en.html (accessed February 5, 2007). Paul VI, in his historic letter of February 8, 1971, to Patriarch Athenagoras, described the Orthodox Churches as being in "almost complete communion" with the Church of Rome: "Nous rappelions qu'entre notre Eglise et les vénérables Eglises orthodoxes existait déjà une communion presque totale, bien qu'elle ne soit pas encore parfaite, résultant de notre commune participation au mystère du Christ et de son Eglise" (http://www.vatican.va/holy_father/paul_vi/letters/1971/documents/hf_p-vi_let_19710208_patriarca-athenagoras_fr.html [accessed February 5, 2007]). See also John Paul II, Wednesday general audience address for the Week of Prayer for Christian Unity, January 17, 1979: "La Chiesa cattolica ha instaurato in questi ultimi tempi fraterni rapporti con tutte le altre Chiese e Comunità ecclesiali,

rapporti che vogliamo continuare e approfondire con fiducia e con speranza. Con le Chiese ortodosse d'Oriente il dialogo della carità ci ha fatto riscoprire una comunione quasi piena, anche se ancora imperfetta. È motivo di conforto vedere come questo nuovo atteggiamento di comprensione non si limiti solamente ai maggiori responsabili delle Chiese, ma penetri gradualmente nelle Chiese locali, poiché il cambiamento dei rapporti sul piano locale è indispensabile per ogni ulteriore progresso" (http://www.vatican. va/holy_father/john_paul_ii/audiences/1979/documents/hf_jp-ii_aud_19790117_it.html, accessed February 20, 2007). The Congregation of the Doctrine of the Faith, in its June 30, 2000, "Note on the Expression 'Sister Churches,'" eschewed the term *sister churches* when referring to Orthodox Churches in relation to the Church of Rome; see http://www.vatican.va/roman_curia/congregations/cfaith/documents/rc_con_cfaith_doc_20000630_chiese-sorelle_en.html (accessed February 5, 2007).

17. See Athens News Agency, "Archbishop Christodoulos to Postpone Vatican Visit," October 11, 2004, http://www.greeknews online.com/modules.php?name=News&file=article&sid=2087 (accessed February 5, 2007); and Phyllis Zagano, "Grant Her Your Spirit: The Restoration of the Female Diaconate in the Orthodox Church of Greece," *America* 192, no. 4 (February 7, 2005): 18–21; translated and published as "Ortodosse all'altare," *Adista* 16 (February 26, 2005).

18. The orphanage, Birds' Nest, is located in Jbeil (Byblos), Lebanon, and is headed by Armenian Archimandrite Paren Vartanian. The deaconesses there belong to the St. Gayane sisterhood. For a history of Armenian women deacons, see Abel Oghlukian, *The Deaconess in the Armenian Church: A Brief Survey* (New Rochelle, NY: St. Nersess Armenian Seminary, 1994).

19. Notificazione delle Congregazioni per la Dottrina della Fede, per il Culto Divino e la Disciplina dei Sacramenti, per il Clero, 17.09.2001, http://www.ratzinger.it/documenti/notifica zionedonnediacono.htm (accessed February 5, 2007):

"1. Da taluni Paesi sono pervenute ai nostri Dicasteri alcune segnalazioni di programmazione e di svolgi-

mento di corsi, direttamente o indirettamente finalizzati all'ordinazione diaconale delle donne. Si vengono
così a determinare aspettative carenti di salda fondatezza dottrinale e che possono generare, pertanto,
disorientamento pastorale.

"2. Poiché l'ordinamento ecclesiale non prevede la
possibilità di una tale ordinazione, non è lecito porre in
atto iniziative che, in qualche modo, mirino a preparare
candidate all'Ordine diaconale.

"3. L'autentica promozione della donna nella Chiesa,
in conformità al costante Magistero ecclesiastico, con
speciale riferimento a quello di Sua Santità Giovanni
Paolo II, apre altre ampie prospettive di servizio e di
collaborazione.

"4. Le Congregazioni sottoscritte—nell'ambito delle
proprie competenze—si rivolgono, pertanto, ai singoli
Ordinari affinché vogliano spiegare ai propri fedeli ed
applicare diligentemente la suindicata direttiva.

"Questa Notificazione è stata approvata dal Santo Padre, il
14 settembre 2001."

The signers were Cardinals Joseph Ratzinger, Jorge Arturo
Medina Estévez, and Dario Castrillón Hoyos, at the time prefects
of Doctrine of the Faith, Divine Worship and the Sacraments, and
Clergy, respectively.

20. "Le Diaconat," *La documentation catholique* 23 (January
19, 2003): 58–107, at 107 (emphasis added; my translation). The
commission maintains the singular "order" found in *Catéchisme de
l'Église catholique.* The English-language canon law (cc. 1008–1054)
uses "orders," and the *Catechism of the Catholic Church* (chap. 3, no.
6) uses "holy orders." The original ITC document was also published in Italian as "Il diaconato: Evoluzione e prospettive," *Civiltà
Cattolica* 154 (2003) I: 253–336. For a discussion of this document,
see Phyllis Zagano, "Catholic Women Deacons: Present Tense,"
Worship 77 (2003): 386–408.

21. See Janine Hourcade, *Les diaconesses dans l'Eglise d'hier et*

de demain (Saint-Maurice: Saint-Augustin, 2001), 21, citing *Il Regno*, July 19, 1985.

22. Martini called for "l'ordinazione delle donne al diaconato, almeno…" at the European bishops' synod in 1999. See Sandro Magister, *"Vade retro, Concilio," L'Espresso*, February 17, 2000. Others assumed to support the notion at the time were Timothy Radcliffe, OP, then Master of the Order of Preachers; Cardinal Karl Lehmann, bishop of Mainz; John R. Quinn, retired archbishop of San Francisco; and Cardinal Pierre Eyt, archbishop of Bordeaux (d. 2001). Cardinal Hume died a few months before this synod.

23. Vangheluwe asked for women deacons during his 2003 *ad limina* meetings. See John L. Allen, Jr., "Belgian Bishop Asks Vatican to Consider Female Deacons," *National Catholic Reporter*, November 28, 2003.

24. "Bartholomew said that there were no canonical reasons why women could not be ordained deacons in the Orthodox Church." National Conference of Catholic Bishops, "News about the Eastern Churches and Ecumenism," *SEIA Newsletter on the Eastern Churches and Ecumenism* 5 (February 1996), 1, reporting from "Genève: Visite du Patriarche oecuménique en Suisse," *Service Orthodoxe de Presse* 204 (January 1996): 3.

25. The principle states that observation alters the reality being observed. Werner Heisenberg's collaborator Niels Bohr termed this the Heisenberg Indeterminacy Principle, and developed a complementary theory that reality has a dual nature, wave and particle, and that we can perceive only one side of that nature at a time. Together these theories are known as the Copenhagen Interpretation and form the foundation for quantum theory.

26. Cardinal Joseph Ratzinger, "Biblical Interpretation in Crisis: On the Question of the Foundations and Approaches of Exegesis Today," Erasmus Lecture for the Rockford Institute Center on Religion and Society, St. Peter's Lutheran Church, New York, January 27, 1988, http://www.catholicculture.org/docs/doc_view.cfm?recnum=5989&longdesc (accessed February 4, 2007). Toward the end of the lecture, Ratzinger cited Thomas

Aquinas: "The duty of every good interpreter is to contemplate not the words, but the *sense* of the words" (Thomas Aquinas, *Super Evangelium S. Matthaeum Lectura*, ed. Raphaelis Cai [Turin: Marieti, 1951]), 358, no. 2321; see Maximino Arias Reyero, *Thomas von Aquin als Exeget: Die Prinzipien seiner Schriftdeutung und seine Lehre von den Schriftsinnen* (Einsiedeln: Johannes Verlag, 1971), 161.

27. Benedict XVI, *Deus Caritas Est* (December 25, 2005), http://www.vatican.va/holy_father/benedict_xvi/encyclicals/doc uments/hf_ben-xvi_enc_20051225_deus-caritas-est_en.html (accessed February 5, 2007).

28. "In the rite of Episcopal ordination…[the bishop] promises expressly to be, in the Lord's name, welcoming and merciful to the poor and to all those in need of consolation and assistance" (*Deus Caritas Est*, no. 32, citing *Pontificale Romanum, De ordinatione episcopi*, no. 43).

29. Ibid., citing the Congregation for Bishops, *Directory for the Pastoral Ministry of Bishops: Apostolorum Successores* (Vatican City: Vatican, 2004), 212–19, nos. 193–98; http://www.vatican.va/ roman_curia/congregations/cbishops/documents/rc_con_cbish ops_doc_20040222_apostolorum-successores_it.html (accessed February 4, 2007).

30. While Benedict named only four women in the entire encyclical—Louise de Marillac (1591–1660), the patroness of social workers who founded the Company of the Daughters of Charity; Teresa of Calcutta (1910–97), foundress of the Missionaries of Charity; Mary the Mother of Jesus; and Elizabeth, her cousin—the subject of women's ministry permeates the document. See Phyllis Zagano, "The Revisionist History of Benedict XVI," *Harvard Divinity Bulletin* 34, no. 2 (2006): 72–77.

31. There are over 30,000 lay ministers, mostly female, in the United States. This number reflects only those paid lay ministers working over twenty hours per week. In 1990 approximately 40 percent of lay ecclesial ministers were women religious. That proportion dropped to 28 percent in 1997 and 16 percent in 2005. See David DeLambo, *Lay Parish Ministers: A Study of Emerging Leadership* (New York: National Pastoral Life Center, 2005), 19, 44.

32. Phyllis Zagano, "Women Religious, Women Deacons?" *Review for Religious* 60 (2001): 230–44. See also Vatican II, Decree on the Appropriate Renewal of Religious Life (*Perfectae Caritatis*), and Paul VI, *Sacrum Diaconatus Ordinem* 32, which provides for deacons within religious institutes. Anecdotally, at least, women religious in developing countries show a great interest in ordination to the diaconate.

33. There is deep ecclesiastical traction against preaching by laypersons. Typically, the presider is to preach: "The homily should ordinarily be given by the priest celebrant" (Sacred Congregation for Divine Worship, *General Instruction of the Roman Missal*, trans. International Commission on English in the Liturgy [Washington: United States Catholic Conference, 1977], 42); however, laypersons may preach at Masses for children, according to the Sacred Congregation for Divine Worship (Directory for Masses with Children [October 22, 1973], no. 24, http://www.catholicliturgy. com/index.cfm/FuseAction/DocumentContents/Index/2/SubInd ex/11/DocumentIndex/477 [accessed February 6, 2007]). Later, eight dicasteries reiterated the prohibition against lay preaching: "The homily…must be reserved to the sacred minister, priest or deacon, to the exclusion of the nonordained faithful, even if these should have responsibilities as 'pastoral assistants' or catechists in whatever type of community or group. This exclusion is not based on the preaching ability of sacred ministers nor their theological preparation, but on that function which is reserved to them in virtue of having received the sacrament of holy orders" (Congregation for the Clergy, "Some Questions Regarding Collaboration of Nonordained Faithful in Priests' Sacred Ministry" [August 15, 1997], no. 3, in *Origins* 27 [1997]: 397–409, at 404). In 1987, the Pontifical Commission for the Authentic Interpretation of the Code of Canon Law responded negatively when asked if the diocesan bishop could dispense from the requirements of canon 767.1, which reserves the homily to the priest or deacon. See John P. Beal, James A. Coriden, and Thomas J. Green, ed., *New Commentary on the Code of Canon Law* (New York / Mahwah, NJ: Paulist Press, 2000), 929.

34. Canon 351.

35. Cardinal Giacomo Antonelli, papal secretary of state (1848–76), is widely considered the last lay cardinal, although he received orders up to the diaconate. See Frank J. Coppa, *Cardinal Giacomo Antonelli and Papal Politics in European Affairs* (Albany: State University of New York Press, 1989).

36. This event is recounted in Phyllis Zagano, "Catholic Women Deacons: Present Tense," *Worship* 77 (2003): 386–408. I was the questioner.

37. Vatican II's *Lumen Gentium* initiated the restoration of the permanent diaconate: "It may well be possible in the future to restore the diaconate as a proper and permanent rank of the hierarchy" (no. 29). See also Pope Paul VI's *motu proprio Sacrum Diaconatus Ordinem* (June 18, 1967), which permitted episcopal conferences to request permission of the Holy See to ordain celibate and married men as permanent deacons: http://www.vatican. net/holy_father/paul_vi/motu_proprio/documents/hf_p-vi_motu-proprio_19670618_sacrum-diaconatus_en.html (accessed February 6, 2007). The U.S. National Conference of Catholic Bishops made that request in April 1968, and the first U.S. deacons were ordained in May and June 1971. The permanent diaconate was universally restored by Paul VI's *motu proprio Ad Pascendum* (August 15, 1972) http://www.vatican.net/holy_father/paul_vi/motu_proprio/documents/hf_p-vi_motu-proprio_19720815_ad-pascendum_it.html (accessed February 6, 2007).

38. Cipriano Vagaggini, *"L'ordinazione della diaconesse nella tradizione grèca e bizantina,"* *Orientalia Christiana Periodica* 40 (1974): 146–89, at 151. The suppression of the first commission study is mentioned in Peter Hebblethwaite, *Paul VI: The First Modern Pope* (New York: Paulist Press, 1993), 640.

39. CDF, *Inter Insigniores*, October 15, 1976, http://www.cin.org/users/james/files/inter.htm (accessed February 27, 2007).

40. "Let it be plainly stated that women are icons of Christ, *Imago Christi*, in every essential way. There is a natural resemblance between women and Jesus Christ in terms of a common humanity and participation in divine grace. To teach otherwise is a pernicious error that vitiates the power of baptism. The naïve

physicalism that reduces resembling Christ to being male is so deviant from Scripture and so theologically distorted as to be dangerous to the faith itself." Elizabeth A. Johnson, "Responses to Rome," *Commonweal* 123.2 (January 26, 1996), 11–12, at 11.

41. John Paul II, *Ordinatio Sacerdotalis* (May 22, 1994), no. 4, http://www.vatican.va/holy_father/john_paul_ii/apost_letters/documents/hf_jp-ii_apl_22051994_ordinatio-sacerdotalis_en.html (accessed February 27, 2007).

42. The 1 Timothy text is contemporaneously understood to indicate women deacons. See Jennifer H. Steifel, "Women Deacons in 1 Timothy: A Linguistic and Literary Look at 'Women Likewise…' (1 Tim 3.11)," *New Testament Studies* 41 (1995): 442–57.

43. Benedict XVI's interview with Bayerische Rundfunk, Deutsche Welle, ZDF, and Vatican Radio at his summer residence at Castelgandolfo on August 5, 2006, was conducted in German and translated by the Vatican: http://www.dw-world.de/dw/article/0,2144,2129951,00.html (accessed February 4, 2007). See also "Pope Says Church Not a String of 'Nos,'" *New York Times*, August 13, 2006.

44. Benedict XVI, "Women Did Not Abandon Jesus," catechesis at the general audience, Vatican City, February 14, 2007, http://212.77.1.245/news_services/press/vis/dinamiche/c0_en.htm (accessed February 27, 2007). In the first Christian communities, Benedict went on to say, "the female presence was anything but secondary." St. Paul "starts from the fundamental principle according to which among the baptized 'there is no longer Jew or Greek, there is no longer slave or free, there is no longer male and female.'" Furthermore, "the Apostle admits that in the Christian community it is quite normal that there should be women who prophesy, in other words who pronounce openly under the influence of Holy Spirit for the edification of the community." Therefore St. Paul's subsequent assertion that "women should be silent in the churches" must "be relativized," said the pope, and he explained that "the problem…of the relationship between these two apparently contradictory indications should be left to the exegetes."